# HOME BY THE SEA

### THE SURF SHACKS & HINTERLAND
### HIDEAWAYS OF BYRON BAY

To the people of Byron Bay,
past, present and future.

Thank you for making this place what it is,
and preserving its infinite beauty,
for contributing to its heartfelt community
and enhancing its creative spirit.

# HOME BY THE SEA

## THE SURF SHACKS & HINTERLAND
## HIDEAWAYS OF BYRON BAY

### NATALIE WALTON

Hardie Grant

BOOKS

We would like to acknowledge the Traditional Owners of the Country on which this book was created, the Arakwal People of the Bundjalung Nation, and the Traditional Owners of Country throughout Australia, and recognise their continuing care for and connection to land, waters and culture, while paying our respect to Elders past and present.

# Introduction:
# Love where you live

CAVANBAH
from Bundjalung, meaning 'meeting place'

COMMUNITY
from the Latin *communitas*: 'public spirit'
from the Latin *communis*: 'common'

When there are so many beautiful places to live in the world, what's the ongoing appeal of Byron Bay? Although it's a small town on the east coast of Australia, its name is known to many across the globe. And it has also become one of Australia's most popular places to visit, and live.

Perhaps, it's because there is something beautiful that can happen when you create a home in Byron Bay. The idea of where you live expands. It becomes less about inhabiting a building, and more about being part of a greater environment and a wider community. It doesn't matter if you live in town, or the hinterland, there's a constant sense of connection to nature, from the country lanes that lead to the coast, and the undeveloped beaches that stretch wide, to the homes that can hear or see rumbling waves or rolling hills. There is an endless array of places to discover: swimming holes, waterfalls, creeks, lakes and lagoons, walking trails, forests and national parks. However, a significant proportion of the population tailor their lives to spend as much time as possible in the surf!

Ask any local what makes this place special and inevitably you will hear the answer: 'community'. But what does that really mean? In part, it is the benefits of living in a small surf town or sleepy hinterland village. Children can roam freely. Friends are like extended family. Business owners become part of your network. And then there are all the little acts of kindness and goodwill that are part of daily life, such as neighbours sharing produce and shop owners buying each other's wares. It reveals itself in the roadside stalls with honesty boxes, community kerbside libraries and village halls that host weekly pizza nights.

When you live in a small community, everyone is connected in some way. Status doesn't work the way it does in the city. When your children go to the same school, and you shop at the same grocery store or market, or are out on the waves, there is little place for ego. Life is better when the focus is on common ground and the greater good.

Simply put, locals are happy to be here and grateful to call this place home. Living in Byron is generally a choice. People don't have to move here for a job or school. More likely, they have tried to find work so that they can stay—or created their own. In part, this explains how Byron Bay has become the birthplace of many brands that have attained significant success on a global stage. The town is a hub of creativity and entrepreneurship in many fields, from food to fashion, interiors and design. And locals support locals, as evidenced by the wares on display in these pages.

As with so much of life here, the creation of homes developed in response to the climate and the availability of resources. For many years houses were traditional cottages for the local farming community, beach cottages built in the 1950s and sixties when longboard surfers migrated to the region, or timber treehouse structures built during the 1970s, when alternative communities formed in the hills. Regardless of the structure, maximising airflow remains key: keeping cool in the long hot summers and dry during sub-tropical storms.

Similarly, furnishing homes has always been a matter of necessity. When this area was still a series of small beach towns or hamlets in the hills, furniture was made, bartered, traded or bought second-hand. To this day, there are still many exchanges made between creatives and brands. It is a circular economy of goodwill that helps maintain the good vibes.

But, while the beaches might be the initial drawcard, there is some other magic at play that keeps the locals grounded and nourished. And it begins in the hinterland. The stunning surrounds were shaped by the remnant core of a volcano, which formed the ranges that have a major impact on the area's weather systems, as well as producing the fertile soil that feeds the region (there's a farmers' market almost every day of the week). It is known to the local Bundjalung People as Wollumbin, 'fighting chief of the mountains', a sacred site. When British explorer James Cook took safe anchorage at Cape Byron in 1770, he named the 'remarkable sharp-peaked mountain' on the horizon Mount Warning. Being able to see the mountain range from the surf at The Pass, and from some of the other white beaches that line the coast, is one of the unique topographical features of the area.

Byron Bay and its surrounds are not just breathtaking in their beauty, but also mythical. They have been home to the Arakwal People of the Bundjalung Nation for more than twenty thousand years. Nguthung is the all-seeing Creator, his resting place is called Nguthungulli and now known as Julian Rocks, an important habitat for the diversity of marine life such as *bubayeh* (sea turtle). Also, often seen in the surf is the dolphin, totem of the Arakwal women, who believe that once they leave the land, their spirits return to the dolphins. When you see these graceful sea creatures off the coast, you know you're watching the ancestors of the Arakwal women gliding through the water. The men's totem is the sea eagle, and you can often observe him gliding around the cliffs hunting for fish. The totem of the people is the carpet snake, which can be found throughout the region, at the beaches and in the hinterland. Totems are sacred and central to their way of life.

Cavanbah, as Byron Bay was originally called, has always been a place to come together and share abundance and knowledge. Traditionally, it's an important meeting place for visiting Bundjalung People to gather for important ceremonies and share the abundance of the mullet run each winter. These large gatherings enabled the trading of cultural resources, stories, songs and dances. However, after European settlement, as the renamed Byron Bay grew, the local Aboriginal People weren't allowed in town, and they were moved on. They settled along the Tallow Beach area so they could remain on their homelands. Arakwal Bundjalung woman Delta Kay is a descendant of the people, including her grandparents, who lived at Tallow Creek. After a period of living in Melbourne, she returned home to be here with her family. Byron Bay is her home, physically and spiritually. It is an honour that she shares her story in these pages.

Creating a home is in large part related to how we connect to our environment, community and history. There have been waves of migration since European settlement in the late 1800s—from the cedar cutters to the whalers, and the arrival of surfers and a counterculture that has mostly managed to keep rampant development at bay. There are many here who have fought long and hard to keep the Byron region the special place that it is. We are wise to remember the protesters, the peace-makers and the passionate creatives who have helped shaped this culture and community. Without the natural environment, this area is a shell of itself. Without the diverse community, the region loses its unique character.

The intention of this book is to get to the heart of what it means to create a home in the Byron Bay area, encompassing not only the beachside suburbs but the villages in the hinterland, each of which has its own character. On the following pages are stories of people who have lived here their whole lives, and those who are newer arrivals. But with each account is a respect for this land, for the original people, and for preserving the spirit of this place that we are fortunate enough to call home.

# Author's note

Although, in many ways, Byron Bay has come to represent a coastal idyll, we cannot lose sight of its history, its social problems, and the impact that humans have had on its natural environment. While its azure waters and white sands beneath the watchful gaze of Wollumbin are the drawcard for many, those who decide to stay a while or create a life here should pause to remember the past, and choose to create a better future.

Its history is filled with incidents that warrant greater awareness. In the 1850s a massacre of the local Indigenous People took place south of Suffolk Park. The iconic Cape Byron lighthouse that opened in 1901 was built on Walgun, a place of ceremony and initiation for Aboriginal men, which was destroyed in the process. There are also significant cultural sites, such as the ancient shell midden at The Pass, which was surveyed in 1994 and found to be more than a thousand years old. It provides important insights into the history of the people and local fauna. While the area is monitored, general awareness is lacking. With the growing popularity of the region comes rising rent that rivals that of big cities. Homelessness has become a huge problem, particularly for older women.

The natural environment has suffered, too. Over the years the cedar-getters logged the land, the dairy farmers cleared huge tracts of what remained and the discovery of gold on the beaches led to twenty mining leases on Tallow Beach in 1870. Sand mining continued until 1968, destroying dunes and changing the landscape forever. Similarly, industries related to whaling and abattoirs also left their scars. It wasn't until the early 1970s, when mining and meat processing had ended, that the face of Byron started to change.

In recent years there has been positive progress due to the tireless work of the local Indigenous People. In 2001 Arakwal Elders signed an historic agreement with the NSW Government to protect Country. The Arakwal Indigenous Land Use Agreement (ILUA) led to the formation of Arakwal National Park, with joint-management decision-making and employment for generations to come. In 2003 Arakwal ILUA was awarded the prestigious Fred M Packard award for distinguished achievements in wildlife preservation by the International Union for the Conservation of Nature.

Earlier, a 1979 student gathering and anti-logging protest at Terania Creek resulted in a new World Heritage area, now known as Protesters Falls. There are many such incidents, and measures have now been taken to preserve the beauty of this place. Awareness leads to greater accountability and a better place that we can all enjoy.

Stories teach us about the past and help create a better future.

Knowledge is key.

Housing affordability is a huge issue in this region. A donation from the proceeds of this book has been made to Fletcher Street Cottage. Also, as this book was about to go to print devastating floods had a huge impact on the Northern Rivers, and some of the people in this book were directly affected. The community came together in unprecedented ways to help those in need. A donation from proceeds was also made to the Bundjalung Community Flood Relief by Koori Mail to help those in rural or isolated Bundjalung communities.

# GYPSY CREEK BANGALOW

## SOULFUL COTTAGE

Past verdant green rolling fields and turn-of-the-century
homesteads on large parcels of farmland sits Bangalow,
a quaint country town with palms lining its main street.
The town's name is said to come from an Aboriginal word,
bangalla, meaning a low hill or a kind of palm tree.
It's a place where well-maintained Federation buildings
house clothing boutiques, organic produce stores
and an old-school pharmacy, all espousing a slower
and simpler way of life.

# LOUELLA BOÎTEL-GILL

'Nature is a massive part of living in Byron.
The trees, the beaches ... being totally immersed in
nature. And the people choose to live here for all of
these reasons. They really want to slow down and
take care of their lives. You get a lot of like-minded
people who are all here for the same reasons.'

*Louella and daughter Chilli
in their hinterland cottage.*

It's a long way from the English countryside to the Byron Bay hinterland and yet, of all the places interior designer Louella Boîtel-Gill has lived in Australia, including years spent in Melbourne and Sydney, this is where she feels most at home.

'There's something about the land that makes me feel I've come home,' she says. 'I grew up in the English countryside, in the county of Hampshire, and driving along some of the roads in the hinterland, with the trees towering overhead in an amazing green canopy, has the same sort of feel as English country lanes. I love driving in this area. It's really therapeutic. It feels as if I've just landed somewhere that's heaven.'

Louella has a penchant for vintage cars, including a 1985 Citroën 2CV and a 1976 Land Rover Series 3, known affectionately as 'the frog'. She is often seen driving through Bangalow on her way to pick up daughters Chilli, fifteen, and Indigo, fourteen, from school, to Federal to visit a local tile merchant, or to Belongil Beach to walk her beloved Irish wolfhound kelpie cross, Lewis. Her cars are recognisable in an instant. As is her home.

While we are visiting, a Sydney friend, originally from France, walks in through the front door. 'Oh, I thought this must be your place,' she says, in her lilting accent. 'It is just your vibe.' The blue Dutch barn door and rusted peace sign, which Louella designed, are clues. This brief moment encapsulates not only Louella's warm hospitality but also what it's like to live in Bangalow, a small and friendly country town. It's the type of place where neighbours pop in unexpectedly, and impromptu dinner parties are all part of the flow.

'I have met so many people here of amazing substance—grounding people,' Louella says. 'I feel like I've come home in terms of the people that I'm around, too.' One of her closest friends is Kimberley Amos of The Atlantic, a Byron boutique hotel. When Louella first bought her home, a hundred-year-old timber cottage, she was still living in Sydney and flew up to Bangalow every other weekend to give the place a coat of paint. When she landed there would often be a message from Kim, showing a photo of a pizza and bottle of red wine. 'We had this Friday night ritual that we would eat pizza, drink red wine and paint the house,' Louella says.

Louella bought the cottage in 2018 at the end of a week-long stay in Byron. At the time she had been looking to buy a place in Sydney, but on her last day

in the area, she couldn't resist an 'open for inspection' sign on a small timber cottage. As soon as she arrived at the front steps, the charm of the house—and the owner—won her over. Jan had owned the place for fifteen years and was sad to let it go, wanting to find someone who would love and care for it as much as she had. As it turned out, one of Louella's friends was an old family friend of Jan's, and had stayed in the home's gypsy caravan when it had been on Jan's previous property. That connection, and Louella's assurances that she would nurture the house and not tear it down, helped secure the deal. Louella was soon bouncing back and forth between Byron and Sydney, holiday-letting the cottage on the weeks when she wasn't in town.

Two years later a phone call forced Louella's hand. Her daughters were both offered a place at a local Steiner school that had a long wait list; the catch was that she had only three days to make a decision about whether to enrol them and make a permanent move to the area. At the time, her ex-husband, Mark Tuckey of the eponymous furniture brand, had just finished his lease on a shop in Avalon. 'All the stars aligned,' Louella says. 'It took a little bit of persuasion to get him into the idea.' But Mark made the move north too, buying a property only a ten minute drive away, allowing their daughters to spend alternate weeks with each parent.

It has been a good move for Louella in many ways. 'Work has gone completely crazy,' she says. 'I find it really interesting that, while Byron is known for its neutral palette, there's been such a huge response to the way I use colour in my interior design work. Every project I do, people are open to being playful with colour. Up here, you have that inherent past of funny old hippie houses and quirky homes that people have cobbled together, which perhaps gives the sense that you can be more playful.'

When it came to making changes to her own home, Louella was sympathetic to the style of the house, while adding her colourful signature. Functional changes were made, such as straightening and widening the front steps, and opening up the kitchen. Sunrooms were adapted to become a bathroom and two en suites in deep shades of blue. The gypsy caravan, which she painted green to blend with its bush backdrop, was extended to add double-bed bunks. This house has allowed Louella to reconnect with her love of mixing old and vintage pieces with new cabinetry. 'That mix has strengthened,' she says. For many years, when she was designing furniture for Mark Tuckey, her spaces were simpler. But Louella is a nester at heart.

'Home is everything,' she says. 'It tells the story of the life I've lived. It's full of memories, and that's why all my funny things are important to me, because they piece together my story.'

'HOME TELLS
THE STORY
OF THE LIFE
I'VE LIVED,
AND THAT'S
WHY ALL MY
FUNNY THINGS
ARE IMPORTANT
TO ME, BECAUSE
THEY PIECE
TOGETHER
MY STORY.'

# CASA PAMPA
# SUFFOLK PARK

## UNDER THE PAPERBARK GUMS

On the slow road south of Byron town, nestled between
Cosy Corner and Broken Head, you'll discover Suffolk Park,
a small community comprised mainly of beach bungalows.
Take a turn towards the hills and you will find a low-rise home
that slowly reveals itself and traces the history of its owners,
who have moved continents to call this place home.

# VICTORIA AGUIRRE

'There is an instant connection to nature here, with access to both the beach and the hinterland. This area has some kind of magic, a beautiful energy. We are lucky to call this place home.'

*Victoria and Carl, with dog Poncho, alongside a bookcase inspired by her grandfather's home in Argentina.*

Buenos Aires and Byron Bay might seem worlds apart but these two cultures have found a synergy in the home that Argentinian Victoria Aguirre has created with partner Carl Wilson. The couple met in Chile, when she was on a photographic assignment and, after striking up a connection, travelled through South America together before moving to Carl's home on the Gold Coast in Australia. On her first weekend in the country, Carl took Vicky camping in Byron Bay. 'I fell instantly in love with the area,' she says. 'It was seriously an energetic thing that made me feel this was the place for us to start a life together in Australia.' However, it took her three years to convince Carl to move down from the Gold Coast, just over the Queensland border.

The couple made the move after their homewares business, Pampa, was up and running, and they had outgrown their two-bedroom apartment. Initially, they lived in Bangalow, a small country town fifteen minutes' drive from Byron. 'We absolutely loved that experience—the slow-paced country life among cow paddocks and creeks but close enough to work and the beach.' They have since moved to Suffolk Park, which is slightly more suburban, but their yard backs onto paperbark bushland, making it feel private and green.

'Our life changed so much since moving to Byron. It's much easier to disconnect and relax, being submersed in nature, and the general lifestyle is easier going and a lot simpler,' Vicky says. Professionally, their business grew on a much faster trajectory after the move. 'We put much of that down to the honest love and support of our community here. Byron is so special in that sense—there's a deep understanding of what it is to support local, and that understanding and support can be everything for a small business like ours.'

While Vicky was able to connect with the local Argentinian community after their move, having a locally based business also helped them to meet a lot of like-minded people who are now good friends. Many of them also have small businesses or are clients. 'For us, moving to Byron was the right move and we have not once doubted our decision,' Vicky says. 'Everything started flowing from that point onwards.'

With work so busy, it was important to create a home that felt like a retreat. 'Our home, we like to think, has a lot of soul,' Vicky says. 'We've put so much love into it and we can feel it when we walk in.' Viewed from the road, the house is a simple 1990s brick-

and-tile, single-storey house, inconspicuous among its suburban neighbours. 'It may not have the high ceilings that we would like, but once you're through the front door it really opens up to something that wouldn't be expected,' she says. While they had to work within a tight budget, and couldn't make structural changes, they have imbued warmth through their use of colour, texture and personal decorative objects.

The appeal of the house is its proximity to the beach and access to bushland from the back gate, which makes the place feel private. The couple spend a lot of time in their backyard with their chocolate Labrador, Poncho, and with friends. Sitting around a firepit in the yard with a glass of wine, while watching the sun drop down through the paperbarks and listening to the screeches of the yellow-tailed black cockatoos, is a part of their weekly routine that they cherish.

'I love the energy of Byron, especially at sunset, for some reason,' Vicky says. 'The views of Wollumbin (Mount Warning) with the sun kissing its back and the ocean in the foreground have become an image of what home feels like. For me, being a photographer, it's all about light and observing small moments during a sunset in different natural areas in and around Byron.'

Both Vicky and Carl enjoy spending time at the beach, too. Carl is a keen surfer and Vicky enjoys the sea life—the dolphins and annual migration of whales making their way across the water. 'It is so very different to the big city life that I lived in Buenos Aires and on my grandparents' farm in Argentina,' she says. 'I love them both, but they are just so very different and not comparable.'

Their home strikes a balance between the two cultures of Australia and Argentina. 'We knew, when designing our home, we wanted to maintain the earthy palette of Pampa because it feels calming for both of us, and for me it reminds me of my home back in Argentina,' Vicky says. 'Pampa means "fertile earth between mountains" in Quechua (a South American indigenous language).' The couple's home represents their loves and the objects they treasure. It's also about embracing natural light and nature. The best of both worlds.

'OUR HOME, WE LIKE TO THINK, HAS A LOT OF SOUL. WE'VE PUT SO MUCH LOVE INTO IT AND WE CAN FEEL IT WHEN WE WALK IN.'

# LAS PALMAS
# MYOCUM

## IN THE VALLEY OF FIELDS

Snug in the foothills of the Nightcap range is a tapestry of
fields that are home to dairy farms and pockets of houses.
Don't be in a hurry though: you might have to wait for cows
to cross the road. But do stop at roadside stalls or take a
moment to watch the setting sun over a golden patchwork.

# SALLY McGARRY

'Living in Byron means we are home.
It is our community; where we are raising
our children. It keeps us inspired, challenges
our perceptions, and grounds us.'

*Sally at Las Palmas, which
references Fenner House, an
iconic mid-century home that her
grandfather commissioned.*

While Sally McGarry has lived in Byron for most of her adult life, when it came to creating her dream home she looked to her past; specifically, to an iconic home that her grandfather had built. It is the home where her family still live today, in Canberra's Red Hill. Fenner House was commissioned by Sally's grandfather, renowned scientist Frank Fenner, and designed by Australian architect Robin Boyd. It is now heritage listed for its post-war mid-century style.

The idea of bringing this home to life in a new way, and within a different environmental context, became possible when Sally, a town planner and project manager, and her husband, Matt, an electrician and large-scale solar specialist, found a six-acre block of land for sale in Myocum. This area, on the western side of Byron Bay, nestles in the foothills of the Nightcap mountains.

'We instantly fell in love with the open space, the hinterland view and the sunset orientation of our parcel of land,' Sally says. 'Every time we came to visit the site, there was a feeling of release, as if the weight of the world was being lifted. We knew this place was the one the moment we arrived; the deal was made the next day over a handshake with the farmer who owned the land.'

Sally moved to Byron when she was eighteen to attend university nearby. Growing up, she had spent her time between Canberra and a beach house on the far south coast of New South Wales. 'I loved surfing and the ocean, so permanently moving to a coastal location was always on the cards for me,' she says. Her university course of coastal management was chosen to secure a life by the sea.

Sally has raised her family here and established a long career in town planning and project management. 'The laid-back lifestyle keeps me in the area, no matter how busy life gets,' she says. 'A surf or some contemplation at the beach will always reset me.'

Byron has changed a lot over the years, Sally says. When she first arrived it had more of a hippie vibe. It was quite a transient place, too. In her early years, friends would come and go. However, once she had children, she was able to build lifelong friendships with a group of like-minded women. 'We all feel so lucky to call this place home and raise our children with a real sense of community and family.'

While Sally spent most of her twenties working and studying, and went back to do two more university

degrees, she has also developed a passion for property and real estate. 'I started buying and selling property in my early twenties and it's something I've been fortunate enough to keep doing in this area,' she says. 'I can see my path changing, now I'm focusing on my own small developments, with a mindset on eco communities and sustainable development principles.'

Before buying the land in Myocum, Sally and Matt lived in Suffolk Park, with the ocean just a step away. They sold that house to create Las Palmas, which is now home for their three boys—Jasper, eleven, Duke, nine, and Sonny, five. The design process started with DUO Architects taking cues from Fenner House's clean modernist lines, passive orientation and connection to landscape.

Las Palmas is divided into two separate wings— one public and one private—with both orientated to capture picturesque sunset views, a gentle breeze and maximum sunlight. The entry foyer was designed to act as a physical connection point of the wings, and a social connection area for family and guests. The elongated roofline and large expanse of glazing reflect Fenner's lines, with the two pavilions lying long and low in the landscape. Highlighting the family's love of water, Las Palmas features an infinity-edge swimming pool nestled in the hillside, connecting the outdoor entertaining zone to the sunset and rolling hills beyond. 'It's a playground for our boys by day and a perfect setting for cocktails in the evening. The pool acts as an ever-changing element of the home,' Sally says.

'We love the simplicity of the house and its connection to the surrounding land,' she says. 'We find it a place that is both grounding and inspiring.'

'WE ALL FEEL SO LUCKY
TO CALL THIS PLACE HOME
AND RAISE OUR CHILDREN
WITH A REAL SENSE OF
COMMUNITY AND FAMILY.'

*Matt and Sally, with sons Duke,*
*Sonny and Jasper.*

At home with

———————

# THE CERAMICIST
# ANNA-KARINA ELIAS
## NEWRYBAR

'I am a mother and an artist, and I live with my border collie, Roman, on a twenty-two-acre hinterland property that I bought in 2006. My four children live away from home and visit when they can. I spend my days taking care of my property, which includes biodynamic practices, gardening, growing and a lot of mowing. I am planning to renovate my existing home, and build a second dwelling that will be called the 'garden house', and am in the middle of building a studio. I am currently researching sustainable building practices and, in between all of this, I make and exhibit art.

'I came to Byron Bay twenty years ago. I was stressed, tired and had gone through a health crisis. I came for a holiday for a week and right then and there I decided to change my life. My children and I were very young and I wanted us to be in nature and live creatively and free, without the need to conform to social expectations. I wanted to get out of Sydney and to experience a simple and beautiful life.

'I didn't know anyone here. I don't need others to give me the courage to do anything. My priority was my children. I wanted to create a life that was healthy and poetic for them. Byron was bliss. The town was quiet and slow. I opened a bookshop in Bangalow and met many people. Parents used to leave their children on the rug reading a book and they would have a coffee next door. It was a very small town.

'My daily life is now very simple. I start with coffee and light some incense. I check what the weather is doing and whether I need to do something to the property; that could be my whole day. If it's market day, I'll go to the farmers' market in Mullumbimby. On weekends I take my dog for a walk and a swim. Depending on what I'm working on regarding my art, I might be researching, sculpting, writing or any one of other activities my practice might need.

'I love Byron. I love the landscape, the ocean, the undulating hills, the green grass and trees, rivers and creeks. I love the air and abundance of produce. Bundjalung Country has a strong sense of self. It requires you to be present and respectful and hold space for the ancientness of it. The traditional owners are wise, humble and strong, with over twenty thousand years of inhabiting this area. They keep their traditions and culture alive to pass on so as to take care of Country. I feel honoured and privileged

# 'I WANTED TO CREATE A LIFE THAT WAS HEALTHY AND POETIC.'

to live here. Byron Bay will always be home. I have come to love this land and ocean, its powerful energy, and I love my silence and the gentle pace of my life.

'I started working with ceramics ten years ago and it has taken me on an incredible journey of self-discovery. The intention of my practice is to make my voice clearer to myself. I do not desire to make my ideas understood by everyone. My work is a way of understanding who I am and a way to process my emotions and neuroses, to communicate visually what I am unable to articulate. I want to understand the human condition, our beliefs, myths, stories and the symbols we create. I use recurring themes of water, women, silence, fragility, flora and fauna.

'Creativity is storytelling.

'Byron is a long exhale.

'Home is a library.'

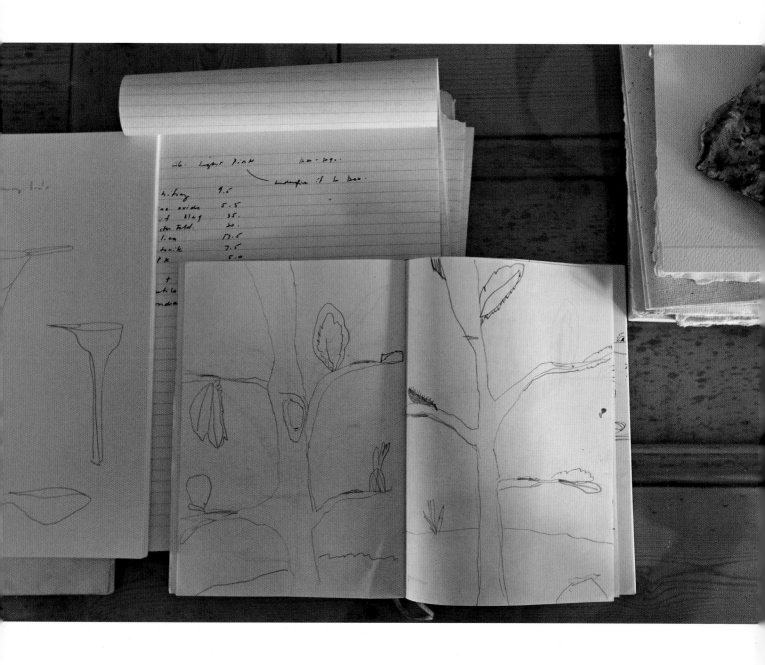

# THE CREEK CABIN
# UPPER WILSONS CREEK

## HIDDEN IN THE VALLEY

Drive through Mullumbimby—known as the biggest little town
in Australia—up and along a meandering road, and into the
valley of the Wilsons River. Pass farms, and fruit trees planted
by the locals. Feel the humidity rise and listen to the sounds
of birds and bush. Immerse yourself in ancient forests and
bathe in creeks and swimming holes. It's time to slow down
and appreciate the majesty of nature.

*Jessica and Reuben on the deck of the*
*cabin they have renovated together.*

# JESSICA BLUME

'Byron Bay gives me a sense of home that I haven't really found anywhere else in the world. It has a feeling of freshness. The water is so turquoise and the sand is so white. There is a constant influx of new people and new things and it has the bright feeling of a summer morning before it gets too hot. It is enlivening, and grounding at the same time.'

When Jessica Blume was growing up in the Byron area it was fairly common that, after finishing school, young people would leave for worldly adventures in big cities and far-away countries. That was certainly her experience. Jume—the name friends call her, and that she has used for her own fashion label—moved to study in Melbourne, a city known for its European look and feel, as well as its design scene.

During her time in the great southern city, Jume began an apprenticeship of sorts, working in various roles as a design assistant while she was studying. She painted pots, wove lanterns and assisted a ceramicist. 'It gave me the skills to know that I could do it myself and start my little label,' she says. 'In Melbourne I used to live in other people's houses and build other people's businesses. Now I'm doing it for myself.'

Every summer Jume would return to Byron, and more and more she didn't want to leave. 'I got really sad having to go back, because the summers here are so much fun. I had just launched my clothing label and started to realise that I could work from anywhere.' However, a relationship break up was the tipping point for her moving back home in 2017. 'I needed

some time to recover and rest, and it was Reuben who made me stay,' she says. 'I would have been somewhere else by now.'

Jume and her partner, Reuben Bryant, who studied conservation science and works in bush regeneration, both grew up in the Northern Rivers region. At one point they lived on the same street in Byron, but didn't know each other until they met one day in the surf. As their relationship blossomed, the couple bonded on trips to Indonesia and Sri Lanka, as well as through a joint love of surfing. In September 2019 they bought this house in Upper Wilsons Creek with Reuben's father.

Jume learnt about the house while she was on a trip to Bali. Reuben called and said he and his dad were buying a run-down place that was going to take years to fix. Did she want to be involved? Jume had always dreamt of having a forest cabin in Wilsons Creek, where she used to visit the swimming holes as a child with her mum. 'I hadn't even seen it, but, without hesitation, I said yes,' she says. 'By the time I got back from Bali, it was happening!'

While the house had a lot of charm from the outside, and sits close to a creek, it required major work.

It had been built of hardwood and cedar in the 1970s as a one-storey cabin and then renovated into the existing house in the late 1980s. The couple later learnt it had been a communal house, the setting for raucous dinner parties, and the haunt of visiting poets and artists from Melbourne. 'He was a healer and she was a writer or musician,' Jume says of the previous owners. 'It was a fun place, a home for parties.' However, in recent years it had been abandoned to squatters and left to fall apart. 'It was just a bare room and a broken piano,' she says. 'There was no kitchen and no bathroom. There were creatures living here. The doors were locked because it was so wild inside. It has come a long way.'

When the couple first moved in, they spent months cooking on a camp stove and taking bucket showers. Fortunately, they have been helped by their fathers—Jume's is a carpenter, while Reuben's is a plumber. 'I had never lived with my father before,' Jume says. 'It was just us and our dads and that made the project so sweet. Every week we were together.'

Since then, they've built a deck and grown a vegetable garden. They also bought a sailing boat, which they've restored. Surfing continues to be a big part of their life, too. While the waves keep them content and connected to the local landscape, having a community of friends has been a huge factor in remaining in the Byron region. When Jume moved back home, she had one good friend who had moved back at the same time. Since then, about forty friends have moved here. Many returned from overseas—from New York, London, Berlin—and from other parts of the country during the pandemic.

'I wouldn't have lived here in the past,' Jume says. 'There weren't enough cultural things to keep me here, instead of the city. Now there are.' She cites great restaurants and bars, as well as the surf culture. 'Byron has everything I loved about the city, in terms of food and events, and yet it's in nature.'

However, unlike her experience of the city, where life can be competitive and judgmental with a feeling of 'tall poppy syndrome', Jume finds the Byron region very freeing. 'Everything feels possible and everyone is super-supportive of what anyone does.'

'We might have left by now,' Jume says. 'But then Covid happened and I don't think I would have wanted to be anywhere else but here. We worked on the garden, surfed every day and built Toko, the shop. That has been really rewarding, because we have brought all the things that we missed from living in cities. We brought it all here.'

When she's home, Jume loves making coffee and pancakes and watching friends swimming in the creek. 'I love the creek being right here, and being nestled in between the mountains.'

'Home for me is somewhere I can feel safe and calm and grounded,' she says. 'I really value the one day a week I spend picking flowers for the vases and slowly making a complete reflection of myself in my home. It's my insides turned outwards.'

'BYRON HAS
EVERYTHING
I LOVED ABOUT
THE CITY...
AND YET IT'S
IN NATURE.'

# QUANDONG COTTAGE SKINNERS SHOOT

## TUCKED AWAY BEHIND TOWN

Once part of the 'big scrub', a sub-tropical forest developed
over 25,000 years, the diverse woodlands that covered much
of the Northern Rivers were cleared by cedar-getters,
who felled trees for quick wealth. In steep areas, the largest,
most valuable logs were slid down 'shoots' to flat land below.
The practice gave rise to many place names in the
Byron region, including Coopers Shoot, McLeods Shoot
and Skinners Shoot, a secluded nook that is now home
to farms and rehabilitated tracts of land.

# ZANA WRIGHT

'I love Byron's community of people, committed to questioning the narrative by which we are supposed to live our lives, and trying to live closer to what feels right in their hearts and bodies. I love that one can experience thriving nature and wild beaches cheek to cheek with world-class creative output. I love the crazy dichotomy of living in a place where the most image-obsessed influencer culture in Australia rubs up against one of the most earthy, tree-hugging, free-loving communities around.'

*Zana in the off-grid home she designed and built.*

There is a strong spirit of working creatively to make a life in the Byron region possible. Adult children build on their parents' land, and friends work collaboratively to keep alive the dream of being able to live here. And so it was for Zana Wright, an architectural designer, and her partner, Sam Jolly, a carpenter, who live on Zana's parents' property in Skinners Shoot with their two-year-old daughter, Lumi.

After growing up in the New England area of northern New South Wales, studying in Sydney, Berlin and Aarhus in Denmark, and coming and going for work, Zana settled in the Byron area in 2015. 'My decision was mostly based around having family here at a time when I was in a transition, but also the wide range of amazing surf breaks, and the community of open-minded folk,' she says. 'As I grew up on an isolated farm in the mountains, the city never felt like my natural habitat. Living in the bush again allows my body and soul to feel at ease.'

Since arriving in Byron, she has moved around her parents' land, gradually upgrading from a tipi in their garden to a converted cow shed and now the house where she lives with Sam and Lumi. Creating this home helped reignite her passion for residential architecture.

'This place became a manifesto of sorts, and has gone on to generate most of my future work.' It's a house that she designed with her friend and previous collaborator Alice Nivison and was built mostly by the hands of friends and family, including her father and Sam, as well as Balanced Earth builders.

The aesthetic of Quandong Cottage was designed around the materials available on site and in the surrounding region. All the timber was grown in north-eastern New South Wales. The earth for the rammed earth walls came from a local quarry; the stone for the retaining walls from a nearby farm. The hoop pine plywood ceiling was grown and manufactured just over the state border in south-east Queensland. The earthen floor in the bedroom was made from clay sourced from the site excavation, mixed with local sand and sugar-cane mulch, which is a by-product of local industry.

The couple rent the land on which their house is built from Zana's parents. 'It's cosy having my parents, siblings and also some good friends of ours all living in different dwellings on the property,' she says. 'We visit one another, share meals and work on property projects on a fairly regular basis. It's also

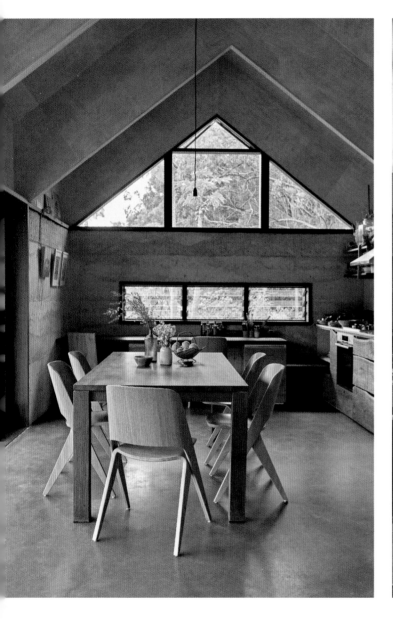

been wonderful having everyone's support while we raise our young daughter.'

The region's subtropical climate influenced the design of the house: two pavilions stitched together by an outdoor dining room, with an external bathroom at one end. 'I love the way we have to pass between indoors and out every time we move between spaces. It connects us to the rhythm of the seasons, changes in weather and the sounds of all the surrounding creatures.'

An added appeal is that the house is not precious. 'The imperfections of its natural material palette allow the chaos of daily life to blend in,' Zana says. 'It doesn't show much dirt, because it is literally built from dirt itself, with rammed earth walls and an earthen floor.' The house is only sixty square metres in area, with just two key rooms, which means it needs to function well and connect to the great outdoors. One pavilion 'room' is the kitchen, dining and living area, while the other is the bedroom, with the bathroom on the exterior.

'I love waking up in the morning, facing east to the rising sun, and gazing at the beautiful dawn landscape through the big square window at the foot of our bed. I love having a vegie garden right next to the kitchen and pottering in there each morning, picking greens for our breakfast. I love how the passive solar design of our home, including its northern orientation, thermal mass materials, ideal eave depths and cross ventilation, means it feels cool in summer and warm in winter,' she says.

Zana's life has slowed down and simplified since she moved back here from the city. 'I now live around the cycle of the seasons and the direction of the wind and swell,' she says. 'I remember that feeling of "coming home" when I realised I was able to get about in bare feet absolutely everywhere here without being stared at.'

Friends and community are important, too. 'One special rhythm I have is meeting up weekly with a group of close women friends to do crafting together at a beautiful secret waterside nature spot, from after work until dark. We have been meeting every week for at least five years and it feels really special to have had these continuous relationships through all of our lives' ups and downs.'

It is not lost on Zana that a feeling of long-term stability and security at home is a privilege. 'I don't take it for granted how lucky I am to be able to rent this home from my parents,' she says. But she is paying the goodwill forward too, creating a beautiful home that will one day allow her parents to downsize with ease.

'I LOVE THE WAY
WE HAVE TO
PASS BETWEEN
INDOORS AND OUT
EVERY TIME WE
MOVE BETWEEN
SPACES. IT
CONNECTS US TO
THE RHYTHM OF
THE SEASONS.'

# THE SIMPLE BARN BANGALOW

## HIGH UP IN THE HINTERLAND

Just beyond the small country town of Bangalow is a quiet lane.
It winds its way through a community that lives on common
land, comprising natural forest, creeks and waterholes.
There is freedom of space, as well as a sense of belonging and,
for some, panoramic views of the surrounding hinterland.

# CLAUDIA MARTIN

'Byron means home, community, beauty, lifestyle, good energy and like-minded people. It means gratitude: we're so grateful to be where we are and not for one second do we take that for granted. In many ways we have downsized our life quite significantly and it's so simple now.'

*Claudia with her youngest daughter, Lulu.*

Moving to Byron was always a dream for Claudia Martin, a food stylist who grew up in Sydney. When she was a teenager and at university she used to visit with friends. 'It was always a special spot,' she says. 'It was somewhere I was drawn to and wanted to spend a lot of time.'

After she met her husband, Levi, a school teacher, the couple spent time in the area because his family is from Bangalow. His grandmother lives in Nashua, in the hinterland. 'He has a lot of family history in the area,' Claudia says. 'His grandfather helped to build a lot of the town, doing labouring work.'

Claudia and Levi started their family on the New South Wales Central Coast, about ninety minutes' drive north of Sydney, but began spending a lot more time on the far north coast when Levi's brother relocated with his family. 'For me it was always the dream,' Claudia says. 'All my friends on the Central Coast knew this was where I wanted to live and have a family.'

In 2016, after being contracted to style a cookbook, Claudia decided to put money aside so the couple and their two daughters, Evie, now nine, and Bindi,

five, could rent a house for three months in Byron after she'd finished the contract. 'We did that for a trial period and just loved it,' she says. 'It just felt that it was the right move for us. It made us work towards the goal of that definitely being where we wanted to be.' During that time they met locals who remain their friends today.

After their trial stay, the couple moved permanently to the region in 2017. Other than the few friends from their three-month visit, they didn't know many people. However, they found it easy to make friends at the beach and cafes. 'It's unique here, in the sense that a lot of people don't have the support of family and grandparents,' Claudia says. 'All the mums can count on each other.'

For the first couple of years the couple rented homes in Newrybar and Bangalow. Eventually they found a block of land on which to build their dream house. After renovating a couple of places on the Central Coast, they were ready to build from scratch in Byron. During their trial stay, Claudia had met a friend who lived on the road where she now lives. 'We went for a drive and fell in love with this area,' she says.

*Claudia and Levi with daughters,*
*from left, Evie, Lulu and Bindi.*

When land was available to buy on this parcel, it sold out quickly, while they were still looking at various properties, trying to find the right spot. However, a year later, when they were ready to buy, someone pulled out and they were able to secure the plot. It was lot number three, which was the number on a favourite jar. 'It felt as if I had manifested it,' Claudia says.

As the block was on a new subdivision, it took time for services to be installed. While they waited, the couple travelled in their vintage caravan down the east coast of Australia and went on a trip to Portugal, where Claudia still has family. 'I stayed at my grandmother's house and she had so much render everywhere,' she remembers. 'I really wanted to bring that in. The Portuguese–Spanish feel is culturally what I was brought up with.'

Claudia and Levi had a clear vision for their home-to-be. 'We just kept calling it a simple barn. We really wanted easy living, and an open living space.' The exterior is clad in blackbutt timber and inside the layout has been kept fuss-free. A corridor runs from the front door to the back of the house, where the living room, dining area and kitchen are located. The bedrooms and bathrooms run off the central spine. While the plot is five acres, the size of the house is modest at 180 square metres.

Less important than the size is the feeling that they wanted to create. 'I love how bright and airy it is,' Claudia says. 'With all the windows, we get to enjoy both sunrise and sunset. It's very open, and I love it in that regard.' From the kitchen window she can watch her daughters playing outside, too. Shortly before they moved into the home, they welcomed their third daughter, Lulu, who is now two years old. That first year Claudia travelled between Byron and Sydney for jobs. But now she is more focused on family life

and less on work. 'I've been fortunate that I've been able to stay at home and it has been a good thing,' she says.

Most days Claudia spends time catching up with friends and other mums with young children at the beach. Afternoons are for home projects and time in the garden. 'We spend a lot of time mowing the lawn,' she jokes.

But there is always something to enjoy and be grateful for. 'Byron is just the most beautiful place. No matter how many times we go for a walk or to the beach, it never gets old how beautiful it is. The land, the soil, the scenery around us ... everything feels so rich. That was what we were initially drawn to.'

While Levi wasn't keen on urban living, for many years Claudia enjoyed the perks of the city. But she isn't missing it. 'Byron is the only place in the world I can think of that's got all the things that I feel drawn to,' she says. 'I feel so fulfilled.'

'WE JUST KEPT CALLING IT A SIMPLE BARN. WE REALLY WANTED EASY LIVING, AND AN OPEN LIVING SPACE.'

In the workshop with

———————

# THE FURNITURE MAKER
# MARTIN JOHNSTON
## BILLINUDGEL

'I'm a second-generation cabinet maker who specialises in creating bespoke furniture and architectural joinery.

'I'm a born and bred local. I went to Brunswick Heads Primary and Mullumbimby High School and after a number of years' studying and travelling and trying to figure out what I wanted, my partner and I decided to move back home. That was in 2010. At the time I had $200 in my bank account, a whole heap of ideas, and access to my father's old workshop.

'When we left this area, we left knowing that we'd most certainly be coming home one day. But I travelled with an open mind and half hoped to find somewhere so perfect that I couldn't leave. I didn't expect to find this nirvana when I returned home to the Byron area, but we did. On every corner, on every street. In every village I'll bump into someone I know. Whether that's an old family friend, someone I went to school with, or someone I see out in the surf. It's the sense of community that makes this place feel like home.

'There has been a massive influx of people into the Byron area, especially in the past ten years. I've witnessed both the positive and negative effects of this popularity, but I choose to embrace this change and run with it.

'I had this beautiful childhood when my mates and I would run barefoot through paddocks of golden grass until we reached the ocean. We'd spend all day surfing, fishing and scratching together enough money to buy hot chips from the local shop. I'm constantly reminded of these moments when I see my sons living the same life. I love spending time on the river, paddling my father's canoe, watching all the birdlife or catching fish, and telling my boys the stories of my childhood while we cook over the campfire. We'll wake up slow sometimes and they help us in the kitchen. We'll go surfing or they'll come with me to the workshop, where they can get messy and play with the tools. It's exactly how I grew up. It's where I learned how to be alive, free and creative.

'Nowadays the word "Byron" means a group of towns, rather than one singular township. It's almost as if the other villages have been engulfed by its limelight, for better or worse. The word Byron doesn't reach the places I call home. Places like New Brighton, Billinudgel, Mullumbimby and Brunswick Heads. I take pride in saying their names because they have had a massive role in my life and are where I feel at home. I feel it's my responsibility to connect my children with this landscape and for them to understand that it was once stolen from the Bundjalung People and that these areas didn't always have the Western names we call them today. To teach them as much as I know, as honestly as I can, is so important for their own growth and the general security of this country. And for them, as future custodians of the land.

'I feel deeply connected with this landscape; it's crazy. I understand the weather around me. I feel subtle changes in an instant. I hear and recognise the calls of the different birds and notice tracks and footprints through the scrub. I can smell the different types of eucalyptus after a summer downpour and notice the sand banks shifting with the seasonal longshore drifts. It's within nature where I feel truly alive. For me, it's a sensory overload and, at times, a much-needed reset. It's as if there is some form of energy pulsing through the hills here, and it's always refreshing to tap into it.

'As a second-generation cabinet maker, I grew up with a lot of architects, builders and other creatives visiting the family workshop. I started off building skate ramps and tree houses and eventually took things a little more seriously. I completed my apprenticeship with

my father and left to travel the world. It was during this time that I realised I had gained important skills that most people don't use any more, and I returned home to pursue and refine a career within the design and manufacturing world. To offer this community a service is pure joy.

'Creativity is having the freedom to be me.

'Byron is—it's an honour.'

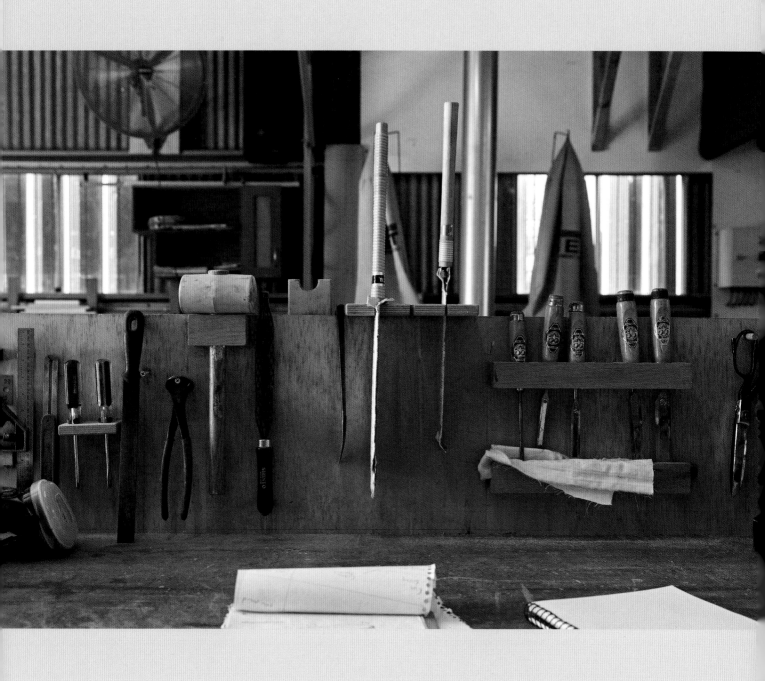

'I HAD GAINED
IMPORTANT SKILLS
THAT MOST PEOPLE
DON'T USE ANY
MORE ... TO OFFER
THIS COMMUNITY
A SERVICE IS
PURE JOY.'

# POET'S CORNER
# BYRON BAY

## A HUB FOR CREATIVITY

There are pockets within Byron town where creativity
and community come together as a welcoming gesture.
The kerbside acts as an offering of poems and posies.
Wander a little further and you might find any number
of community initiatives, founded with the humble idea
that we are better together.

# YVONN DEITCH

'Byron Bay is such a welcoming place. So many people arrive from somewhere else, leaving family and friends behind. Often they travel here for a holiday and don't leave. This was my story, and the story of so many.'

*Yvonn in her Mediterranean-inspired courtyard.*

After living in a large timber house high on the hill in Coopers Shoot, and with all the responsibilities that come with living on a property, Yvonn Deitch was keen to move into 'town', as locals call Byron Bay. She wanted to be able to ride her bike and walk to the shops and cafes. But Yvonn is the type of person who doesn't do anything half-heartedly. Every gesture is considered, and executed with poetic flair. Recently she had the words 'be a poem' tattooed on her forearm, and this sums up her approach to life and creating a home in Byron Bay.

Yvonn was born and raised in Germany, but fifteen years ago decided to take a year off work to travel and see a little more of the world. 'I hadn't taken a gap year and felt it would be wonderful to travel and explore beyond Europe before settling down,' she says. 'After spending six months in Southeast Asia, I was very excited about visiting Argentina. Australia was to be a little stopover, I thought. I met my husband and the father of my children in the Byron Bay post office and never left. It took a lot of courage, after only a few weeks with David, to make the decision to stay in this country. My English was so limited and I didn't know anyone here.'

However, she found Byron to be a welcoming place. 'I love how you can easily start a conversation with a stranger,' she says. 'There is so much eye contact while walking the beaches and you give away smiles freely. That's something you will not find in many places.'

About two years ago Yvonn built a new house from scratch. 'David and I separated, and I am still in awe about the fact that we have been able to build this place together, for the children and me.'

She calls it her 'new old house' because Yvonn wanted it to have the feel of an established home. While their Coopers Shoot house had been large and expansive, she wanted this home to feel intimate and personal for her young children, Matilda, ten, Frida, eight, and Leon, five.

'I always wanted a kitchen nook where the kids, being so little, can snuggle in the morning waiting for breakfast, instead of feeling lost at a huge dining table or elevated on bar stools around a kitchen island,' she says. 'The shower downstairs is more of a kids' car wash with three showerheads, so there is no fighting over whose turn it is, and the sunken bath can fill up and often the kids stay longer and play with Lego. We sometimes hang gum leaves, eucalyptus and lemon myrtle branches in the shower and it feels like a moment in the rainforest.'

The bathroom upstairs pays homage to a run-down French hotel, where Yvonn once stayed in her twenties. 'I love how the northerly wind blows the curtains horizontal,' she says.

There are many personal touches throughout the house, including a tiny door that connects Leon's bedroom to Yvonn's through her walk-in-wardrobe. Matilda has a secret compartment in her bedroom wall, behind a picture frame. 'These are some of the little playful touches you can make when building a home,' Yvonn says. 'I hope the kids will always remember them with a smile.'

Outside, a boat that was saved from the Hawkesbury River has been transformed into a cubby house in the garden. However, not every feature has been designed solely for the children. The courtyard was supposed to be a place to park cars, but has been converted into a terrace overflowing with bougainvillea, and herbs and blooms in terracotta pots. 'We have the most beautiful lunches with family and friends, and it feels like a little European holiday,' Yvonn says. As she knows all too well, each moment provides an opportunity to create beauty in the every day.

'WE SOMETIMES HANG
GUM LEAVES IN THE
SHOWER AND IT FEELS
LIKE A MOMENT IN
THE RAINFOREST.'

# THE BEACH SHACK
# BELONGIL BEACH

## NESTLED BEHIND THE SAND DUNES

Escape to the quieter end of town, and a decidedly slower
pace, where locals walk their dogs and take a quick dip
or cheeky lunchtime swim. Cross the train tracks and
take the only road in, with the creek on one side and the
promise of surf on the other. Almost hidden from view
is one of the oldest houses in the area, lovingly restored,
well-used and treasured by a local family.

# SONYA MARISH

'I love living in a small community and being surrounded by trees and nature. I love the diversity of people, and what this place means in terms of what you can do artistically.'

*Sonya in one of Byron's original beach shacks.*

When you've spent most of your life travelling the world for business and pleasure, sometimes the best type of family holiday is right on your doorstep. And this is how it came to be that Sonya Marish ended up with a beach shack at Belongil Beach, only a twenty-minute drive from the village of Federal, where she lives with her family of five and runs her business, Jatana Interiors.

Sonya and her husband, Anthony Solomon, a general practitioner, moved to the region more than twenty-five years ago when he started working for the Aboriginal medical centre in Casino. 'It was a wonderful move,' Sonya says. 'Although it was very different back then.'

At the time Sonya was working in the travel industry and had a market stall selling unique finds and treasures collected from her travels to remote parts of the world, including Pakistan and Tibet. 'They were quite closed areas back then,' she says. When she moved to the Northern Rivers, Sonya sold her wares at markets across the Shire, but over time she specialised in sourcing antique tiles and eventually creating her own designs for the business.

'I was so excited to be here, out of the city, and loved exploring all this area had to offer, such as yoga schools and tarot card classes,' she says. All the while she continued to travel back and forth for work while raising three children: daughters Jhalia, who is now living in Berlin, and Taya; and son Naraian, who has just finished school.

About six years ago the family stayed at a beach house in Belongil and fell in love with it. Soon Sonya was calling a real estate agent to buy a place. 'He was trying to sell us a modern one down the road,' she says. 'But it wasn't me. So he told me to get into the car and show him what I liked. I saw this little shack. The lovely man who owned it had so much stuff that you could barely see past the gate. That's the kind of place I like, I told the agent. I knew that was the one.'

The owner had tried to sell previously but no one had been interested, despite the house's beach access. 'You couldn't even walk in the house,' Sonya says. 'We had to do a lot of clearing and cleansing.'

While the house is one of the oldest in the area (certainly, one of the closest to its original condition), it wasn't always that way. 'We uncovered the house,' Sonya says. The owner had been born and bred in it and his parents lived there before him. Over the years, timber windows had been replaced with aluminium. There was cork on the ceilings and vinyl

on the floorboards. Sticky contact paper that looked like wood covered the walls. There was plastic cladding all over the exterior. 'We took it back to its bones,' Sonya says. 'We found wood under the contact paper and under the cork. We took out the aluminium windows and knocked down some of the dividing walls.' However, they used the same footprint to start again. 'Someone once said to me, "I've never seen anyone buy an old house and make it look older,"' Sonya laughs. 'We love the fact that because it's so small and simple it's easy to maintain.'

Now it's a place where the family goes to relax by the beach. 'You walk in there and it feels like a holiday. It's our little haven and little escape from our busy life in Federal,' Sonya says. 'We never had the intention of being busy—life in our shire has become busier than we all anticipated.'

While no one lives in the house permanently, it is used daily. Anthony often stops by for lunch during his work break. Naraian will meet friends there and go for a surf. The doors are often open to friends, family and events, too. There have been a couple of weddings in the house and plenty of dinner parties.

'Home is a combination of a sacred quiet space and also a place to entertain our beautiful friends,' Sonya says. 'I love using our home as a canvas to create my own beautiful little world. I love to express who I am here with my colours and unique collectables. This is very much a part of who I am. It's a reflection of all my years of travel and experiences.'

'SOMEONE ONCE SAID TO ME, "I'VE NEVER SEEN ANYONE BUY AN OLD HOUSE AND MAKE IT LOOK OLDER."'

# YALBARUBA
# TINTENBAR

## A HAVEN AMONG THE FARMS

Drive along scenic country roads, past old churches and
roadside stands, with handmade signs and honesty boxes,
selling locally grown produce and flowers. Feel the pace slow
as you pass macadamia and dairy farms. You're only a short
drive from Killen Falls, a remnant of the 'big scrub' rainforest
whose timber attracted European settlers to the area,
as well as Byron's world-famous beaches.

# THE FEWSON FAMILY

'We are grateful to be here, in the Bundjalung Nation. Creating a home here has been the result of a huge creative journey, embarked upon as a family.'

*The Fewson family (from left): Purslane, Jane, David, Hannah with Sorrel, and James.*

What began as a year-long trip around Australia in an old converted fire truck in 2014 turned into a whole new life for Jane and David Fewson. They started their journey in Fremantle, Western Australia and now reside close to Australia's most easterly point, about 30 minutes south-west of Byron Bay.

The couple sold their Fremantle home, which they had renovated after moving from Broome, to embark on their trip. When they arrived at Mullumbimby Showgrounds they planned to stay for only a few days, but soon found themselves looking at real estate. 'We were attracted to this place because its climate and community are so gentle, compared with the harshness of Western Australia. We felt at home instantly,' Jane says. They soon fell in love with the property Yalbaruba, meaning 'place of healing' in the language of the local Indigenous People of the Bundjalung Nation. The former macadamia farm sits on twenty acres in Tintenbar. 'The house was at the back of the property away from the road and we knew we could turn the old 1970s build into something special,' she says.

When the renovations began, their daughter, Hannah, moved up north from Sydney, where she had finished her degree in anthropology, to help. She got a job at the local pub and met James, who grew up in nearby Eureka. 'When we got engaged and started having babies there was no question we would stay in the area, as I love it too,' Hannah says.

Now Yalbaruba is also home to Hannah and James' children, Purslane, aged two, and Sorrel, one month, as well as their blue heeler, Bean. Len the bull terrier lives in the main house with Jane and David.

When we meet the family they are all sitting on the verandah of the main house, drinking cups of tea together before the day begins, in a nod to Jane's English heritage. David and James excuse themselves to continue working on their newest building project, a low-set mid-century style concrete house on the property. After we chat, Jane runs errands before returning to do regeneration work by the creek, and Hannah returns to her house, a Queenslander that has been relocated to the front paddock of the property.

After Jane and David bought the house in 2014 it underwent a major renovation. The original house was a seventies brick-and-tile two-bedroom rundown

home with swirly brown carpets and orange glass. The living quarters were upstairs, and at ground level were two carports. Jane and David, who have renovated many homes over the years, envisaged a new concept for the house, effectively doubling its size. The former carports were enclosed to create an open-plan living, dining and kitchen area. Upstairs there are now four bedrooms and two bathrooms. The red brick has been clad in golden cypress, which is slowly greying. The roof was changed to a lower pitch and hidden behind a parapet, to create the appearance of a flat roof line.

David, a carpenter and builder, also made a lot of the furniture, including all the beds and the dining table, which was crafted from timber that was part of the original roof. Other furnishings are vintage finds.

With the main house renovations complete, there has been more time to enjoy their new life in this part of the country. 'Life is wonderful here, mostly because of having two families living side by side,' Hannah says. 'Also, our decision to rip out all the macadamia trees on the property—due to the sprays and our desire to take a different direction with the land— created the opportunity to design and build our accommodation spaces.'

Most recently, they have completed Paddock Hall, a cabin-style building that embraces traditional carpentry techniques. And work remains underway on 107R, the concrete house with a vegetative roof. Both projects are run as a family business. 'This allows us to all pursue passions and work part-time on projects we choose,' Hannah says. 'We give reverence and recognition to the Nyangbul People, on whose land we live and work, and feel so thankful and connected to this property the more we engage with it.'

When they are not working on the property, they spend weekends together, relaxing. Every Sunday afternoon they have a big barbecue and invite their neighbours. 'Usually, a few other locals who live nearby will drop in and have a drink around the fire as the evening goes on,' Hannah says. While they don't venture into Byron often, Hannah loves the view of the mountains from the beach. 'And I love the access to great food and wine, and gigs. That feels particularly special to me, having grown up in Broome, where living in the country generally means going without such things. We love the hinterland, the little villages, all with their own characters, and the scenic drives between them all.'

For the most part, they enjoy being at home. 'We love the space around us to create whatever we want, the quality of soil to grow whatever we want, and the kindness of our community.'

'WE FEEL SO
THANKFUL AND
CONNECTED TO
THIS PROPERTY
THE MORE WE
ENGAGE WITH IT.'

On Country with

———————

## ARAKWAL BUNDJALUNG WOMAN DELTA KAY
BYRON BAY

'I am an Arakwal Bundjalung woman, passionate about sharing, preserving and protecting local Aboriginal culture through guided tours and programs with my business, Explore Byron Bay.

'My family raised me on Country, mainly at Belongil Creek and Suffolk Park. I went to Melbourne to get my early years qualifications in the mid-1980s, immersed myself into the strong Koori culture and had a mob of kids, then one day I woke up to a strong calling to come home. My heart and spirit returned me home nineteen years ago. I'm back, and I'm never leaving again.

'I came home and worked hard with the Ballina Bundjalung Community and loved every opportunity to learn from incredible Elders such as Aunty Nancy Walk and Aunty Nita Roberts for several years. Then I started my Aboriginal Educators position with National Parks and Wildlife Service (NPWS). A passion to teach my culture on our traditional lands has been my inspiration. Being nominated to sit as chairperson of Cape Byron Trust committee has been an incredible experience: continuing our Arakwal Elders' vision of caring for Country through our award-winning joint management with NPWS.

'Every job I have held has enabled me to share my passion for education and Aboriginal culture. I'm now at an age when I want to continue this work but choose the jobs I want and the hours I want. It's time for me to slow down and be on Country more.

'We are proud Arakwal People of the Byron Shire; we belong to the Bundjalung Nation. Arakwal People are Native Title holders of the Byron Shire area. Our Elders' vision is to protect Country, for our people to have rights to use Country, and we share parts of our culture with the wider community so they understand and look after Country like we do. The high volume of tourism is harming Country—it is important that we work together to protect this special place for our future.

'I have a deep sense of contentment being on Country. My relationship with the land is in my blood, my heart, my bones. As a traditional custodian I have an ongoing duty from my mother and her mother to garima (look after) Country.

'After waking in the morning I call out to the ancestors then head out to harvest bush tucker. I spend time observing changes, birds, animals and the seasons.

This is my meditation time. I love spending my mornings with my partner before I start any meetings, school programs and tours. I also sit on many committees, working with education and cultural issues. I believe being in control of my time has been the best decision to keep me happy and healthy.

'Byron is where I belong. It is Cavanbah (meeting place) where I can make an impact for our community, our culture and our people.

'Home is peaceful, joyful and safe for my family and me.'

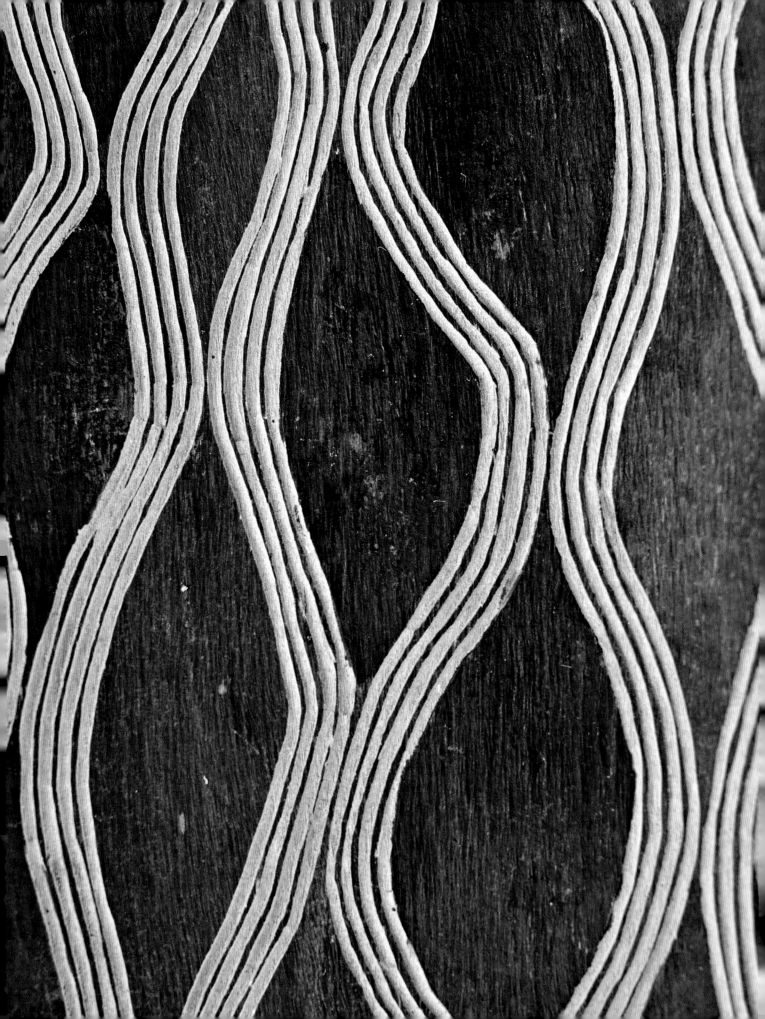

'ONE DAY I
WOKE UP TO
A STRONG
CALLING TO
COME HOME ...
I'M BACK, AND
I'M NEVER
LEAVING AGAIN.'

# CURATORIAL HOUSE SUFFOLK PARK

## A SLEEPY BEACHSIDE POCKET

What was once a modest gathering of dwellings in
a sleepy offshoot on the southern side of Byron Bay has
now become a burgeoning suburb, home to young families
seeking easy beach access and a quiet life away from the
tourists in town. Beachside offers the best of both worlds:
a short stroll to the white sandy beach of Tallows
and easy access to native bushland.

# ALEX BENNETT

'As I was raised here, Byron has always felt like home. It's comfortable and familiar. I have lots of memories; it's been the base for most of my life experiences and I can't picture myself anywhere else. It is also absolutely stunning, so I feel very lucky to be part of such a special place.'

*Alex in a home that's within a whisper of the ocean.*

Interior designer Alex Bennett knows a good thing when she sees it. After moving fourteen times in the four years since her daughter, Scout, was born, she had her eye on a block in Suffolk Park, a ten-minute drive south of Byron Bay. At the time she was living in another house in the area, which she often ran as a guesthouse. 'I have always loved this block,' she says. 'It's one of the largest in Suffolk. There's another on the opposite corner that's the same size, but this is north facing.'

Having started her renovating journey at the tender age of eighteen, and transformed many places over the years, Alex knows that aspect is one of the few things that can't be changed in a home. If you want natural light to flood your living areas, in this part of the world you need a northerly aspect.

While Alex was eyeing off the house, she learnt that the owners would only agree to sell if they found a property in nearby Newrybar that had a macadamia farm yielding a certain tonnage. 'I put in an offer and it took them seven or eight months of looking—it was one of those long-burn deals,' she says. 'In the end they found 110 acres in Newrybar, they bought it, and we bought their place, and the deal was finally done.'

While the block was 1289 square metres of land, the house itself had been significantly neglected and was very dark. But it was a 1980s double-brick home, which held great appeal. The plan had been to give it a freshen up and move on. 'Like always, it ended up a substantial reno and we absolutely love it,' says Alex, who lives in the house with her son, Parker, seven, and Scout.

One of the big drawcards was the home's good layout, which made large structural changes unnecessary. However, a fireplace was removed from the living area and a garage converted into a media room. An office was added to a corner of the living room and closed off by fluted glass doors with custom handles. The original house had slate flooring, which Alex loved, but when the renovation began the slate started to crumble. She couldn't opt for solid timber floors, because of the existing concrete slab, so Alex chose tiles. Lots of white paint helped brighten up the whole space, as did large sliding doors that open on to a timber deck.

Despite the house starting out as a dark place, its natural light is now Alex's favourite feature. 'It is just so bright and airy all day. We spend a significant

amount of time at home each day, which tends to be the way for a lot of families with young kids. I love how comfortable and happy our kids are in the space and enjoy seeing them sharing this with their friends. It's a great house to entertain, as the kids spill out into the yard and we can all sit on the deck, catching up and watching them play.'

Alex enjoys collaborating with local makers and creatives to furnish her homes. When not sourcing vintage pieces, she sketches out designs for friends to make as custom pieces, such as a side table in her bedroom and a burl wood table in the living room. But she is a minimalist at heart. When one piece enters her home, another leaves. 'I edit pieces out,' she says. 'If I get a new piece, I take another piece out.' She also believes in buying once and buying well.

Alex is hands-on when it comes to working on her home. She painted the ceiling in the living room, for example, and at the front of the house she planted an entire garden, which includes coastal varieties such as white pigface (*Carpobrotus glaucescens*) and grass trees (*Xanthorrhoea*). 'I am constantly inspired by the natural environment and landscape in this region, and feel very grateful to be part of this shared experience,' she says.

While Alex is engaged in the work–life juggle of young children at home, there are many sweet moments to savour. The family often see koalas, on the move along the top of the timber fence in the back garden. They can also access a boardwalk through their gate that takes them to a nearby resort for an easy dinner, or wander a bush track to the beach or nearby Tallow Lake. It was a big job to clear the garden, which had been overgrown with shrubs up against the house. Now there is plenty of space to breathe. Simple, just as Alex likes it.

'I AM CONSTANTLY
INSPIRED BY THE
NATURAL ENVIRONMENT
AND LANDSCAPE IN
THIS REGION.'

# SOMA RETREAT EWINGSDALE

## TRANQUILLITY AMONG THE TREES

Take a moment to be still, before you walk down a path
lined with giant bamboo that arches overhead and frames
a geodesic yoga dome. Pass lychee forests and native trees.
Make your way to Mother Fig, who has been nurturing this
space for more than two hundred years, and take a rest in
one of the hammocks that hang from her far-reaching boughs.
Feel the release of your thoughts, and just be.

# GARY GORROW

'Byron is my favourite place on Earth. The mentality here and the beauty of nature are everything for me. There is so much creativity, so many conscious people doing incredible things with their lives and time. It's an inspiring place. The perfect mix of spirituality, creativity, dynamism and opportunity.'

*Gary lives in a small home alongside Soma Retreat that reflects its architectural style but on a smaller scale.*

Listening to your inner knowing is a strong thread that runs through Gary Gorrow's life. It has helped guide him personally and professionally, resulting in the creation of a venture that intertwines his passion for deepening his self-understanding, as well as helping others reconnect with their own consciousness.

Until not so long ago Gary was based in Sydney, where he had been born and raised on the Northern Beaches. 'I had a wonderful life down there. My meditation practice was well-established and very successful,' he says. 'I had strong and long-standing friendships, yet I kept feeling an inner calling to give everything away and move to Byron Bay.' He did just that in 2014.

'It didn't make sense on paper, to throw such a spanner in the works,' he says. 'My life was great, but, as I discovered, when you follow the call into the unknown, wonderful things await you there. My leap of faith has opened up so many opportunities and delights.' Since he moved here, many of his good friends have also made the migration north.

When Gary arrived in Byron he was able to connect with locals who were already friends, thanks to years of travelling to the region. 'It's always been my favourite place in the world,' he says. 'Byron is a very welcoming place; because of that I've formed an incredible number of new alliances. People are so genuine and open in Byron. They come here for a reason: to cultivate a quality of life. Like-mindedness abounds, so friendships form very easily and deeply. Since creating Soma I feel that the community and tribe is only increasing. Community and friendship is everything to me.'

Soma is both a home and a retreat space to share with others who want to learn or deepen their self-knowledge through meditation. Gary co-created it with his brother, George Gorrow, who is behind Bali's boutique hotel The Slow, and investor Peter Ostick. When he first arrived in Byron, Gary was on the lookout for a property where he could create his dream retreat. He found this parcel of twenty-two acres in Ewingsdale at the end of 2016. The property was surrounded by cattle farms; however, the previous owner had cultivated lychee fruit trees and a bamboo nursery and plantations. She had also established rainforest in an area where there had previously been mass land clearing.

While much of the landscaping has been maintained, the buildings are almost entirely new. Soma Retreat is the most notable: a new two-storey build for up to twenty guests that incorporates open-plan communal spaces and ten private king-sized bedrooms, each with its own en suite. The main house has been designed to embrace as much natural light as possible, as well as enhance spatial proportions and create a sense of flow. Designed by Indonesian architect Rieky Sunur, the building is clad in timber and galvanised steel and incorporates floor-to-ceiling glass windows, internal gardens and a pond that trickles between indoors and outdoors beneath a glass window near the main entrance. Many of these ideas adhere to the Vastu principles of sacred architecture, part of the Vedic tradition.

Gary lives in a smaller house on the property, affectionately known as 'Baby Soma', thanks to its architectural style referencing the main house. The original hundred-year-old house was full of asbestos and mould, with rats living in the walls. 'It was an absolute disaster before I moved in,' he says. 'Now it's been transformed into a beautiful little home.'

Gary lives a simple life in Baby Soma with his children, Leela and Matisse, when they are not at their mum's. 'I love this home, primarily because I designed it to suit my needs. I spent a lot of time contemplating and planning so that it would be functional for me and my kids.' While it's near the main house, it has privacy and a charm of its own. Either way, Gary is able to make the most of its location. 'The proximity to the surf is massive for me,' Gary says. 'I love being able to strike town easily, but I relish being immersed in the forest, away from all the hustle and bustle.'

For Gary, living in Byron means living life on his terms. And home is a place for peace, pleasure, growth and comfort. Gary also encourages visitors to remember that they're on sacred ancestral land when coming to the region.

'Be mindful of the spirit of this place. Don't seek to bring your needs here, or any pretension, consumerism, judgement—but open yourself up and adapt to this community. Love and respect this place and it will love you back. We're walking a fine line. Byron is fragile and we have to preserve the wonders of this place.'

'I LOVE BEING ABLE TO
STRIKE TOWN EASILY, BUT
I RELISH BEING IMMERSED IN
THE FOREST, AWAY FROM ALL
THE HUSTLE AND BUSTLE.'

# CREAM HOUSE SUFFOLK PARK

## UNDER SHERBET SKIES

Among the tuckeroos, where kookaburras laugh, kids can be
seen running down the street, heading to the white sands of
Tallows to burn off afternoon energy. On the beach, where
whiting and bream can be caught in the fishing channels,
a family heads out under sherbet skies before the full moon
rises shining a light on this life they have created together.

# CANDICE ROSE-O'ROURKE

'Byron is about not compromising on meaningful moments; spending quality time with your loved ones; investing in good produce for your family; and supporting local vendors. Sourcing and collecting your favourite pieces from artists, ceramicists and craftsmen; ensuring your work leaves a positive legacy for the next generation; and, most of all, living a wonderful life that you are brave enough to create.'

*Candice in her home designed for sandy feet and beachside living.*

Candice Rose-O'Rourke has made a living and a life creating products for the beach that encompass both nostalgia and a modern edge. So it makes perfect sense that her home embodies both these elements, too. As co-founder of apparel label Zulu & Zephyr, as well as children's brand Millk, she has created a beachside home that is contemporary but with a nod to the past. With clean architectural lines, warm-toned bricks in the entrance and travertine tiles in the bathrooms, it has a fuss-free coastal aesthetic that is both robust for family living and subtle as a backdrop for her love of art and artisanal wares.

Candice and her husband, Josh, a plasterer (who got to enjoy the satisfaction of plastering his own family home), wanted to create a beacon of stability and security for their children, daughter Zimmy, seven, and son Val, five. It's a little different from their own upbringings. Josh was born in Bathurst and grew up in a bus all along the east coast of Australia. He arrived in Byron Bay in the nineties with his family, living in the bus. And Candice, who grew up in Port Macquarie, would visit the area as a young teenager in her dad's campervan, before relocating at eighteen to study journalism and marketing at the local university. 'As two kids who bounced from bus to rental homes when we were growing up, to have settled and put roots down for our own kids is special,' she says. 'We designed with a mindset that our home had to be suitable for young kids, teenagers and, eventually, us as an old grandma and grandpa.'

After travelling around Australia, and the world, the couple decided Suffolk Park was the community that best suited them to start a family. The satellite beachside town south of Byron offers the best of suburban life—wide, flat streets filled with children riding bikes, scooters and skateboards—alongside one of the region's best beaches, Tallows, as the locals call it. 'We are an ocean family,' Candice says. 'We spend our days sea-side, surfing together or hanging out in the local tea-tree lakes. We have an incredible group of friends who are all talented, ambitious, interesting and successful in their own ways. Our life is built around the beach, year round: what are the winds doing? What's the temperature today? What's the swell doing? The water is incredibly nourishing for our family and it's where our young children can exercise, socialise, explore and connect. You will find us at the beach most days.'

This is the couple's second home in Suffolk Park; they lived in a neighbouring street for a number of years,

their first place together. However, when an old brick house with a large empty yard became available in December 2018, it was too much of an opportunity to let pass. Candice and Josh were keen to build their own home from scratch. They bought the 1450-square-metre block with Candice's sister and co-founder of Zulu & Zephyr and Millk, Karla Rose.

The sisters built their homes side-by-side in complementary styles, albeit with distinct differences. Candice chose an off-white exterior and named her home Cream House, while Karla designed the Kookaburra Residence, inspired by architect Jørn Utzon, as well as by their grandmother's 1970s brick house, and finished the exterior in black.

'The double block belonged to local sisters. When they learnt that my sister and I—together with our partners and children—were hoping to build and settle long term, it resonated,' Candice says. 'We offered the asking price, which they generously accepted before it went to auction.'

Unfortunately, their father was diagnosed with cancer not long after settlement. He moved into the existing brick house on the block to pursue treatment in the area before the families started demolishing, clearing and building. 'He spent his last summer with the children, coming and going on the block. For the last three months of his life, he got to immerse himself with the people he loved in the place where we would settle. While he did not live to see the completed project, we feel him around us, every day watching over us,' Candice says. 'To us, this is not only a project: here is a piece of earth that holds meaning and memory.'

This home allows them to create new memories, too. 'We love hearing the ocean at night, and the northerly winds that blow through the house and garden,' Candice says. 'After being here for a year, I can sense what to expect from the mood and light of each season. I love the northerly winds in summer and the dappled light in winter. We feel safe and protected always.'

The house was designed with spaciousness in mind. 'Hearty brickwork, bold pillars, interior and exterior paving—a bunker-style home filled with light and love,' she says. 'We feel lucky to live here.'

'THIS IS NOT
ONLY A PROJECT:
HERE IS A PIECE
OF EARTH THAT
HOLDS MEANING
AND MEMORY.'

At home with

_____

# THE HERBALIST
# ERIN LOVELL VERINDER
## CLUNES

'I am a herbalist, nutritionist and author of two plant medicine books, *Plants for the People* and *The Plant Clinic*. I live in a church with Noah, a graphic designer and all-round stellar Virgo, who designs books and co-creates all things plant-loving with me.

'I have been coming to this region for over twenty years and had formed a deep relationship with it since I was a teenager, regularly staying with friends up here. They shared with me its beauty, taking me to swim in hidden waterholes and at wild beaches, going to markets filled with community spirit. It left an imprint on me, and called me back. I knew at some point I would call the Northern Rivers home.

'In 2018 we were considering the move and our friend shared that she was leaving this very special church home and it was up for rent. It felt incredibly kismet. We jumped on it, moved within a few weeks and have never looked back. Life got much sweeter for us. We began to work together on creative projects and running my clinic, and I wrote my first two books in this sweet old church house.

'Over the years, many of our friends had relocated north to this region, so we arrived to a warm welcome and a very strong ready-made community, feeling incredibly embraced. This was wonderful, as the previous area we lived in never quite gelled for us in that way.

'Community is everything, and the spirit is so strong here. Bumping into friends at the beach, or an impromptu catch-up at the farmers' market, all of these moments create a sense of place and connection that has been a wonderful balm for us both.

'We both joke that we have never been so busy as since landing here. There is a powerful creative energy in this region—it feels palpable. I became an author here, writing both of my books back-to-back over a few years.

'When we arrived, I revolutionised how I worked, switching my whole clinical practice to an online platform, which has allowed me to work solely from home at my own pace. Noah and I started working together on all our creative pursuits, keeping it in the family, which has been so wonderful. Moving here was the catalyst we were seeking to make over the way we worked and lived, with the intention of spending more time together, to create a flow that matched our desired rhythms and aligned with the vision of our life together.

'Our mornings are slow: breakfast at home or an early swim in the ocean and grabbing a smoothie before heading home. Work days are full, whether I am seeing clients, mentoring, writing, or formulating recipes—it all happens in our home. We both take breaks together, always eat lunch in the garden, and try to break up the time spent on screens with the antidote of more nature time. Living here has helped me feel nurtured and nourished on so many levels. Having the autonomy to work for ourselves and at a pace that suits us both has been healing. We balance our workdays with time in the garden, an ocean swim, time in the kitchen, walks with the dogs, swinging in the hammock under the pecan tree. I have learnt that I can still work hard and create aplenty, without becoming a shell of myself. You will find me weeding garden beds or planting seeds during a work break. I find this deeply relaxing and therapeutic.

'I love this region immensely, since the very first time I came here as a seventeen-year-old who had grown up in the outer suburbs of Sydney. This region shook up my preconceived notions of a regional area. I fell in love with the strong spirit of the land and the open-minded community. I love that it holds so many special free-spirited thinkers and creators, people who care about living the good life in communion with the land. People who appreciate this place deeply and, therefore, want to caretake it. This weaves a palpable community through the region, which I believe is quite unique.

'When we came here, the churchyard was absolutely barren, bar the old pecan tree and a lemon tree. It was a flat plot of red dirt and sporadic grass. We built a very large vegie and herb garden, and expanded it during the pandemic. We always have an abundance of food and medicinal herbs growing, and I make boxes to hand out to my neighbours. If feels special to share with them what we have tended and grown.

'Being a herbalist and nutritionist is a potent way to reconnect with the earth and the bounty that nature-based healing offers us all. For me, it is about communion with nature; there is no separation between ourselves (humans) and nature. Medicinal plants and eating nutritious foods grown from the soil bring us that bit closer to oneness.

'Living here means being part of a caring, connected community, early morning swims, and sun-kissed, salty hair.

'Home is an oasis, our space to be free and authentically us.'

'WE BALANCE
OUR WORKDAYS
WITH TIME IN THE
GARDEN, AN OCEAN
SWIM, TIME IN THE
KITCHEN, WALKS
WITH THE DOGS,
SWINGING IN THE
HAMMOCK UNDER
THE PECAN TREE.'

**Plants for the People**
A modern guide to plant medicine

*Erin L*

ON UNFOLDING

Often healing is not pretty. Sitting with discomfort is not easy. Sometimes you have to break down to break through.

Let's demystify the expectation of always being and feeling the same. Health is a representation of your evolution. It is ever-changing.

You are in motion. You are healing.

# SIGNATURE SPACE
# BYRON BAY

## COASTAL IDYLL

Beyond the breathtaking scenery, Byron has always been
a place of dreamers and doers. In recent years a wellspring
of small businesses have been able to grow at their own pace,
from humble beginnings, away from the bustle of big cities,
to thrive on a global stage. The simple life has infused organic
growth and, fortified by community support, underpinned
the success of many businesses based in Byron today.

# LARA FELLS

'Byron is ever so inspiring. I always feel alive here—
like anything is possible.'

*Lara and newborn baby Jean,
happy at home.*

Just over a decade ago Lara and Matt Fells, co-founders of the clothing label St. Agni, packed everything they owned into their car and drove to Byron Bay in the hope of creating a new and exciting chapter in their life together. The couple had met three years earlier in Tasmania, when Lara was just eighteen and Matt was travelling around Australia, away from his home in the United Kingdom. 'We were young, naive and wide-eyed, packing up our car and driving from Tasmania, without a job lined up or anywhere to live,' Lara says. 'I think my adult life began with this move. Neither of us had lived out of home and I had never had a full-time job. We started St. Agni three years later and slowly grew our little passion project into what it is today.'

When the couple first arrived in Byron they didn't know anyone but found the community welcoming and friendly. At first they both worked in retail, which helped them meet many locals. 'I have never been fast to make friends, and it took over a year to make the good friends I have today,' Lara says.

'My life has completely changed since moving to Byron Bay, having arrived at the age of twenty-one, with little idea of what I wanted to do with my life,' she says. In the past ten years, the couple started St. Agni, which is now stocked in leading fashion stores around the world, bought their first home, married and had their sons, Jude, four, and newborn Jean. Harper the cavoodle is also a valued member of the family unit.

When Lara was eight months pregnant with Jude, the couple moved into their home, which has recently undergone a refresh. At the time, the location of the house held huge appeal. It's only a five-minute walk to the beach and is close to the centre of Byron Bay. However, it's also tucked down at the end of a street and backs onto bushland.

'We were invited to look around the house before it was officially on the market,' Lara says. 'From the front we didn't really like it, but when we walked through the house to the living area we were sold. The open floor plan, the high ceilings and abundance of natural light gave the house a really nice feel.'

The first phase of making the house their own was to pull up the carpet, paint the floors white, and furnish the home in their signature pared-back style of 'less is more'. They also added a pool that overlooks

the bushland. More recently, they have laid oak floorboards and incorporated the same timber in the kitchen and bathroom cabinetry to add more warmth. They also made some adjustments to the floor plan to give the master bedroom a walk-in robe and bigger bathroom, and lifted door heights to accentuate the ceiling height. 'I wanted to give the house a warm, homely feel, while keeping it in line with my minimalistic aesthetic,' Lara says.

But an abundance of natural light is her favourite feature. 'We really wanted to be able to open the house up to the outside as much as possible to really enjoy the sub-tropical climate,' she says. 'I think it's so important to have a lot of light.'

The local environment has a huge influence on them. 'Living in Byron, you can't help but have a relaxed approach to design,' Lara says. 'I find myself drawn to wearing a pair of vintage Levi's and a white tee, and I like open airy spaces and natural materials.'

Ultimately, home is a place where they want to be with family and friends. 'We tend to cook a lot on the barbecue and just prepare a quick salad. My mother is Greek so I've grown up enjoying Mediterranean-style meals,' Lara says. 'During the week Matt and I go into the office most days, as we are really hands-on with the business. On weekends we love going out for breakfast and spending most days at the beach. We like to keep things pretty simple.'

'I love the lifestyle Byron has to offer, and that we can run our business from here and then enjoy the beach at the weekend,' she says. 'It's a very unique place to live. I don't think I could live anywhere else.'

*Matt, Lara and baby Jean at home with Harper the cavoodle.*

'I WANTED TO
GIVE THE HOUSE
A WARM, HOMELY
FEEL, WHILE
KEEPING IT IN
LINE WITH MY
MINIMALISTIC
AESTHETIC.'

# VILLA JALAN
# BANGALOW

## BESIDE BYRON CREEK

Opposite a row of old workers' cottages, Bangalow Parklands and the weir on Byron Creek remains a popular spot for locals to commune, and for children to jump from a rope swing into a freshwater swimming hole. In many ways, this area has always been a meeting hub. The local Aboriginal People fished here, and gathered medicinal plants. In the 1920s The Waterfront, as it was known, was a thriving community space, complete with a public swimming pool, and the venue for carnivals and dances. In recent years it's come back to life, thanks to the creation of a wetlands zone where you can spot a platypus or turtle, have a picnic, walk your dog, and enjoy the community spirit of Bangalow.

# HEIDI DABURGER

'Byron has a calm ebb and flow, but it's also full of energy every season. It's like being part of a global community, because we get to meet so many people from all over the world. Each season they bring a dynamic energy to Byron; however, the place never loses its origin nor identity of familiar characters. That makes me happy.'

*Heidi and Honey at the entrance to a cottage that embraces global influences.*

Life journeys are rarely linear. However, when we look back they often make sense. We can see the paths we have taken and how they have formed the basis of our journey, and ultimate destination. After a life of travel and many years working in the hospitality and design industry, it makes perfect sense that Heidi Daburger has been able to combine her passions at home and in her business. Her company, Ha'veli of Byron Bay, sources antique furniture and homewares from around the world to create experiential interiors.

'I have always known since I was a child all the things I wanted to do—just not the order they were meant to be done in, or have presented themselves in,' Heidi says. 'We should have a favourite list of all the professions and paths we want to explore. It's about building a road so you can travel to the next project.' Heidi has always enjoyed the hunt for a new project. 'I'm a bit of a gypsy. There's always room for another challenge; risks are exciting.'

Her first major renovation in the area was about six years ago, when she created Haveli House, a short distance from where she lives now, just on the other side of Bangalow. In many ways, that cottage created her signature island-luxe style, and has led to a lot

of consulting work on design and interiors concepts, drawing on the pieces that she sources and imports on international buying trips. Heidi's most recent personal project has been transforming a 1940s workers' cottage into Villa Jalan, a bungalow on the fringe of the historic town of Bangalow. It was an opportunity to create a home for herself and a space for a holiday letting, while showcasing the global wares she sources for Ha'veli. The name is derived from an Arabic word, 'haveli', meaning 'private space', that later came to be used in the Indian subcontinent to describe styles of regional mansions and manor houses. To create Heidi's version of a haveli, she begins with a white canvas and layers it with earthy objects and tribal antiques.

'I have always bought and renovated old cottages, no matter what state they're in,' Heidi says. 'The first thing I do is look up at the ceiling and if I can't reach it, it's perfect. It's mine!' she says. 'If you can't jump, you can't grow!'

She bought the house in 2018, attracted to its heritage charm, rear studio, and location overlooking Bangalow Parklands. While Heidi has avoided making many structural changes in the front cottage, she has created significant impact through her use of

furniture and furnishings, installing large-scale antiques from India and Indonesia, such as Indian doors as bedheads. As each piece is unique, they create a bespoke feel that's also timeless.

The studio underwent a greater transformation. What was once an exercise room, complete with dance barre and floor-to-ceiling mirrors, is now unrecognisable. Lining the roof with white painted latte poles has created an island holiday feel, while the use of salvaged railway sleepers (from the nearby Teven Bridge) on door frames and for cabinetry adds an earthy appeal. The neutral palette keeps the elements feeling cohesive.

The look that is recognisable as her own was cultivated during years living in London. 'I spent holidays in Greece and Italy, where I was immensely influenced by architecture and rustic design,' she says. 'The nomadic lifestyle suits me. I feel at home anywhere. It's what you make around yourself. The people you interact with must have substance and interest: people who challenge themselves. But, at the same time, I need community with roots so I can come home from being a gypsy.'

Heidi's family have lived in the Byron Bay area for twenty years as farmers, so this region became a second home for her, even when she was based in other parts of the country. While she grew up in Melbourne, and worked on the Gold Coast in hospitality for many years, she started her importing business selling wares out of a barn on the family farm.

'Since then, Ha'veli has expanded as our community is ever evolving with a focus on creating beautiful homes,' she says. 'There are so many creative people in our region who have supported local business. I'm excited to be part of so many people's homes and lifestyle decisions. The best moments are seeing pieces come alive in people's places.'

Life in Bangalow provides Heidi with a gentle rhythm to her days. She wakes to the sound of birdsong, the sheep across the road or the neighbour's chickens. She takes her beloved dog, Honey, a border collie, to the park and for a swim at the nearby creek. By then, the baker should be ready with fresh croissants. 'It's time to sit and take it all in,' she says. 'Home is a calm place I'm happy to be in. It's at times both happy and hectic, and full of love.'

'I FEEL AT HOME
ANYWHERE. IT'S
WHAT YOU MAKE
AROUND YOURSELF.'

# THE LOCAL JOINT
# BYRON BAY

## THE CREATIVE HUB

Byron has always been a place with a strong focus
on community and collaboration, working together for a
greater good. When your home is a short walk from town,
with its abundance of creative types and local produce,
it would be tantamount to waste not to incorporate
this connection within a living environment. So, step
through the arched gate, past the jasmine vines and through
the cactus courtyard, to find a house and hand-built cabins
that push the boundaries between home and hotel, curated for
comfort, where art is created and curious living encouraged.
Because connection and creativity are the heart of the home.

# CHELSEA WADDELL

'Byron is the perfect balance of grounding energy and stimulating inspiration. Being so close to the ocean allows us to slow down and connect back to ourselves and to each other as a family. The creative community in the shire is something that invigorates and recharges us as creatives. There's a vitality to the texture of the energy here that makes it so much more than a sleepy beach town.'

*Chelsea has returned to her roots, living in Byron Bay.*

Coming to live in Byron Bay felt like a returning of sorts for Chelsea Waddell and her partner, James Lyell. The creative duo, who met in Sydney, had both spent a significant amount of time in the beach town. Chelsea went to the local high school, after spending her early childhood in Bellingen, another small town a few hours south, with a similar alternative vibe. James had been living in Bondi for fourteen years, although he visited Byron frequently. 'We'd only been dating for a few months when we decided to pack up our separate lives and fuse them together in this house in Byron,' Chelsea says. 'Many travels, a big renovation, a baby during a pandemic, and here we are.'

Chelsea has worked in the arts for the past decade, focusing mostly on contemporary fine art, but has recently pivoted towards floral design. 'I love the sculptural element, colour palette and composition of creating a floral arrangement,' she says. James is a musician, music producer and writer, as well as one half of Australian band, Flight Facilities. Together they run Joints in Byron, a boutique accommodation business. 'It's a collaborative, community-focused space that we think is a true celebration of Byron

life,' Chelsea says. Not only do they have two studios available for rent on their property, but they run artist-in-residence programs, workshops and a monthly dinner series. 'We wanted to create a space for ourselves, and the Shire at large, that fostered this need and want for communal and collaborative creativity.'

Since arriving in Byron, the couple have become parents to Louie, now two years old. 'Our daily rhythms have pivoted and adapted to incorporate this new role,' Chelsea says. 'But having built a house together really allowed us to explore this idea of home being a signifier of self. So, although our lives have changed and grown since arriving in Byron, having this space where we can connect back to our intention has been a huge contributing factor to how we've taken these changes on board.'

Their property, located in the heart of Byron town, originally comprised a bungalow typical of homes in the area. The couple wanted to keep the bones and integrity of the building, and its sense of laid-back coastal living. Chelsea describes the home now as 'curated imperfection'. It incorporates a playful conversation between rustic and modern, light and

dark, minimalism and refined elements. 'We wanted the style, both architecturally and design-wise, to complement the ethos of the space: a celebration of communal living, family and community.'

The couple also built the garden studios, allowing their vision for creative collaboration to come to life. During the many stages of the renovation and build, they were involved with every decision. They spent about six months living in one of the unfinished studios, without a kitchen or bathroom, surviving on take-away food and a suitcase of clothes to make sure they didn't miss anything that happened on site. Chelsea was pregnant throughout the whole process and they outsourced all the manual work, as she says that neither of them are particularly handy.

Now that the bungalow, where they live, is finished, they find themselves gravitating towards the kitchen island. It was intentionally positioned in the heart of the home so that whoever is cooking never feels alone. Its central location lets the cook see into the front and back courtyards, listen to a record that's playing in the living room, or have a conversation with the people around. 'And the light is beautiful from morning until afternoon,' Chelsea says. 'There's nothing better than a space that is well lit with natural light.'

While the couple are drawn to different aesthetic styles, their home is a synergy of both, and unified through a neutral palette. 'I believe that it's the small details that make a space feel like a home,' Chelsea says. 'The little collected treasures that reflect who you are.'

It is the special energy of Byron that keeps them enamoured of this place. 'It's something you don't often see or feel in other small coastal towns. It's as if you're right at home and somewhere completely new and exciting both at once,' Chelsea says. 'While there's so much familiarity and ease about living in Byron, the creativity and verve that underlines its history enables you to feel there's always something new to explore or discover. There are a lot of tales to be told here—from the people, the history, the land—and I think when that kind of storytelling is so ingrained into a community and the environment it makes for a pretty special town.'

'I BELIEVE THAT IT'S
THE SMALL DETAILS
THAT MAKE A SPACE
FEEL LIKE A HOME.
THE LITTLE COLLECTED
TREASURES THAT
REFLECT WHO
YOU ARE.'

In the garden with

————

# THE ARTIST
# MEL LADKIN
## SUFFOLK PARK

'I am a mother, daughter, sister, aunty, partner, and proud Awabakal Wonnarua woman with ties to the Githabul Bundjalung People. I share my home, which sits on the land of the Arakwal People, with my husband, Simon, and two children, Jarrah and Kiahn.

'We were pulled to Byron (Cavanbah) in 2006 so our children could be brought up in a smaller community. Having lived on Awabakal Country (in the Newcastle area), it was getting very busy and beginning to feel like an extension of Sydney. My brother lived in Lennox at the time and my parents had been bringing us here for holidays for most of our childhood.

'The transition, moving to Bundjalung Country, was very easy. I work in the environmental sector. The climate is spectacular, the locals welcoming and my partner and I both surf. Having small children just starting school and involved in sports was a perfect way to immerse ourselves into community. Once we landed, finding how I could be of service and participate really helped in assimilating and connecting. I am so grateful to the incredibly supportive people who have walked beside me and been a part of my family's journey so far.

'We have lived in two homes since arriving in the Shire, both in Suffolk Park, which has been a lovely area to raise small people to large humans. Easy for them to ride to school and do after-school sport, then work, as well as having a sense of freedom. I've been caring for Country for most of my life as a bush regenerator by trade and have continued to work in that field for close to thirty years. After arriving here, I worked predominantly for private clients while sitting on the board for National Parks and Wildlife Service advisory committees. I did notice that, generally, people were more aware here of the need to care for our land and environment. It is beautiful to witness people wanting to learn more about where they reside, and being willing to give back to the natural environment by rehabilitating their properties into habitat for wildlife.

'A typical day always starts with a twenty-minute meditation and then an hour's walk on the beach. I generally start work at 7.30 am, a mid-morning paint, back to work until lunch, which is spent painting, and that dance continues throughout the day. I work from home, helping a small not-for-profit, Hands with Hands, as well as doing my bush work. My art practice is all and any time in between.

# 'CREATIVITY IS ESSENTIAL TO MY WELLBEING. IT'S INTUITIVE, MEDITATIVE AND HEALING.'

'Aesthetically, the Northern Rivers is abundant in beauty. The whole caldera area, with its lush remnant rainforests, over a hundred national parks in the region and a seriously stunning coastline—what's not to love? It draws a very eclectic range of people to the area and has a sense of space that you don't get living in a city.

'I have always had an art practice, but only started sharing it over the past few years. I work with ochre and natural earth pigments, and make all my own paints. Having a deep love of soil, geology, the natural environment and, most importantly, my culture guides my work. My practice represents the multi-layered history of our people and our intrinsic connection to Country. I hope it can evoke and resonate the connection to our ancient land and how you walk upon it.

'Creativity is essential to my wellbeing. It's intuitive, meditative and healing. It is my connection to my culture, a way of sharing and storytelling. It brings a sense of peace and lets all else become quiet. Time does not exist when I am in my practice.

'Byron (Cavanbah) is just one part of the incredible Northern Rivers region, which continues to inspire me with its rich diversity, incredible beauty and amazing community. There are so many talented artisans of every craft, as well as amazing humans dotted throughout the area. The biodiversity of the landscape is one of the richest in the country.

'Byron has a population of just over fifteen thousand people and we expand to over two million visitors per year. I do hope, moving forward, we can manage these influxes and continue to manage the complexities of tourism and its impact on housing in the area.

'Home is a feeling of belonging, and feeling safe and nourished by the space you reside in. Being a Cancerian, home is everything to me. I am most comfortable at home, hiding in my shell. Home right now is this place, on Arakwal Bundjalung Country, and I feel incredibly privileged to share it with my partner and adult children. We all feel deeply connected to this place.'

At home with

———

THE AUTHOR
NATALIE WALTON
BINNA BURRA

'Living in Byron has created a sense of freedom like no other place that I have lived. It has allowed me to connect on a deeper level with the most important strands of my life: family, friends, community, creativity and myself. There's nothing quite like surfing alongside dolphins, watching storms rumble across the sky or seeing a golden sunset along the hills to put everything into perspective. I will be forever grateful for the lessons that I have learnt on this sacred land, and in its magical waters.'

'After living in Sydney for most of our adult lives, carving out careers there and starting a family in beachside Bondi, my husband, Daniel Rollston, and I embarked on a tree change in 2015 to a parcel of land, a ninety-minute drive north of the city. And while it was a wonderful experience in so many ways, it also wasn't quite what we were searching for. We missed feeling connected to a critical mass of creatives with an entrepreneurial spirit, but we didn't want to go back to city life. We had contemplated moving further north, to Byron Bay, for almost fifteen years. We finally took the plunge and bought a Queenslander-style timber home in the hinterland in 2018.

'One of the benefits of already living on land was that we had a clear idea about what we wanted from a property. Our last place was on twenty-six acres, which had been overwhelming at times. This time, we found a place on two acres of cleared land, and a much less steep block. The house had hinterland views, a north aspect and enough space for all of us: a family that had grown to include Charles, thirteen, Sabina, ten, Isis, eight and Miles, five. Plus, the property had a garage and storage shed that could be converted into a studio for our homewares business, Imprint House. The owners were a lovely couple in their eighties who had carefully maintained the house for more than twenty years. It was also only twenty minutes' drive to the beach, five minutes to Bangalow and ten minutes to another town with a strong community spirit, Federal.

'When we made the move to Byron, we already had family, friends and contacts living in the area. We will never forget that first week in our new home. We had driven north with our trusty vintage caravan, Atlas, and thrown mattresses on the floor of our new place. In the morning we watched from our kitchen deck as hot air balloons hovered overhead. After dinner that first evening one of our neighbours across the valley had a party, complete with fireworks. It felt like a welcoming signal. A few days later we were offered places for the children at a local Steiner school. And in another couple of days we were asked to join a local retail collective. Almost every day of that first week it felt we were receiving signs that we had made the right decision. It's one that we haven't ever regretted.

'Since buying the property we have made modest modifications to the home. Before we moved in, the walls were painted white and the floors sanded back to a matt finish. It gave us a neutral foundation to add the pieces we have collected over the years that make it our own.

'Life is good here. The children enjoy harvesting mangoes or avocados from the trees, depending on the season. And we enjoy a gentle rhythm to our days, making the most of the beautiful weather and the community of like-minded creatives and entrepreneurs, who want to live a good life and leave the world a better place. This is home.'

'BEFORE WE MOVED IN, THE WALLS WERE PAINTED WHITE AND THE FLOORS SANDED BACK TO A MATT FINISH. IT GAVE US A NEUTRAL FOUNDATION TO ADD THE PIECES WE HAVE COLLECTED OVER THE YEARS THAT MAKE IT OUR OWN.'

About the author: Natalie Walton is an interior designer and stylist, as well as founder and creative director of Imprint House, a concept store and design studio based in Byron Bay. She is the author of several best-selling books, including *This is Home: The Art of Simple Living; Still: The Slow Home;* and *Style: The Art of Creating a Beautiful Home.*

For more, visit nataliewalton.com and imprinthouse.net.

At home with

_____

# THE PHOTOGRAPHER
# AMELIA FULLARTON
## EWINGSDALE

'When I first moved here, I loved that it was still just a small country town. I love the connection to nature you can feel so easily here, I love our community of friends that have been like family to us over the years of raising our kids.'

About fourteen years ago, when Amelia was still a teenager, she had just got back from backpacking around Europe with some girlfriends and didn't want the holiday to end. 'My best friend and I had one weekend at home and then we got in the car and drove north from Sydney,' Amelia says. 'My mum said, "I've only seen you for a day and you're gone already!" We camped in a tent for a while, finally got jobs, found a share house to live in, and never looked back.'

Although Amelia didn't know anyone when she arrived, the transition to living in Byron wasn't difficult. 'We were young and it was easy to meet people in the community pretty quickly,' she says. 'It was completely different to where I grew up, in the sense that I was on my own for the first time, not living with my family. I felt totally free, and I just wanted to have fun. We met many like-minded people in those first few years here.'

Life has completely flipped from that first experience. 'I went from being nineteen, having basically zero responsibilities, living in share houses with lots of friends, to meeting my partner, Al, and building our life together with a career and a family.'

About four years ago they built a house on a 1.5-acre block of land they had bought a few years earlier in Ewingsdale. 'When we found the block we immediately knew we had to get it. We bought within a few days of seeing it,' she says. 'It was so close to the beach but still had acreage, and having space was important to us.'

The house was built on a tight budget and based on the idea of two simple rectangular boxes joined together. Their architect, Davor Popadich, had built a clever, comfortable and affordable home for his family in New Zealand, and that inspired Amelia to want to work with him. The finishes, size of the home and simple layout kept the costs minimal.

Today their home is full of life, with four girls—Arlo, nine, Agnes, six, Ottilie, four, and Una, twenty months—as well as a pony, three chickens and a dog, Secret. 'We love the north-facing aspect and the space around us,' Amelia says. 'The home stays really cool in summer and warm in winter. We love how everything is open to the outside, even the bedrooms. We can see the sky at night, and the trees and birds flying about during the day.'

# 'WE CAN SEE THE SKY AT NIGHT, AND THE TREES AND BIRDS FLYING ABOUT DURING THE DAY.'

About the photographer: Amelia Fullarton is a photographer who uses natural light to capture people and places that evoke emotion. Her work has appeared in *Vogue*, *Harper's Bazaar*, *MilK* magazine and other publications. Her personal projects focus on children's portraits. Amelia is based in Byron Bay.

*I want to thank Natalie for asking me to take the photos for her book. I'm so grateful to have had this opportunity. It has been such a pleasure to have worked closely with her, and I've learnt so much through her skilful eye. To my partner, Al, for always supporting me and being there for our girls when I'm busy working on projects like this. I could not do it without you.*

At home with

———————

# THE DESIGNER
# HOLLY McCAULEY
## BANGALOW

'Byron is familiar faces, a balmy breeze, mosquitoes,
palm fronds on your roof, condensation on your glass of beer.
It's where the ocean, rivers, rainforests and hills converge.
Where the climate differs from postcode to postcode.
And the longest I've ever stayed in one place.'

About twelve years ago Holly McCauley arrived in Byron Bay with a hatchback full of clothes and books, a blow-up mattress and a plan to move closer to her new job in south-east Queensland, an hour's drive away. She moved into the sunroom of a share house with a group of girlfriends, a place where no one owned a key and the whole place was furnished with pieces found at the local op shop. The garage was a meeting place for playing music and talking late into the night. 'Safe to say, I never moved to the Gold Coast,' Holly says.

'I spent the next few years relishing my friends and enjoying all that Byron had to offer for kids in their twenties. These formative years were not only filled with all of the above, but also a growth in understanding of who I was and what I wanted out of life. I recognised the simple pleasures that city life didn't offer me, and felt a growing appreciation of the transformative healing vibes of living in close proximity to nature and friends. Twelve years later, I'm still here, raising my daughters alongside all those girlfriends.'

Today Holly lives in a cosy shack in the country town of Bangalow with husband Nich, an apprentice cabinet maker, and their daughters, Della, five, and Posey, two. They bought a 'renovator's delight' five years ago, sight unseen, on the recommendation of a builder friend.

'We were not renovators, but Nich has touched every inch of our home and transformed it into a place we love that reflects our no-fuss attitude towards fancy things and excess. We pulled out weeds that were taller than us to make room for a deck—a must to increase the usable space in a 60-square-metre home. We ripped up the carpet to reveal a concrete slab, which we polished with a hand grinder. Never again! We clad walls in VJ boards to try to trick the eye into thinking the space was bigger than it was. Our friend hand-built a garden shed for visitors to sleep in. Slowly, we filled the home with art, family heirlooms, books, furniture made by mates, treasures collected on travels and, eventually, two daughters,' Holly says.

'We love that this place is everything we need, and nothing we don't. Every square metre gets used daily. There's no excess, no part of it that doesn't have a use. We are slowly growing out of it, dreaming of adding an extra sleeping nook, or perhaps making a move out of the suburbs to somewhere with sweeping views and more space to run. But for now, it's perfect.'

# 'WE LOVE THAT THIS PLACE IS EVERYTHING WE NEED, AND NOTHING WE DON'T. EVERY SQUARE METRE GETS USED DAILY.'

About the designer: Holly McCauley has worked for many years as a graphic designer, specialising in books and publications. She is also co-founder of Yeah, Nice Gallery in Byron Bay, which opened in 2018.

*Thank you to Natalie and the team at Hardie Grant for trusting me in helping to bring this book to life. Thank you to my dear friend Amelia for her beautiful imagery and to Natalie for reminding me of that special feeling of home.*

# Thank you

This book would not have been possible without all the generous people in this community. They have not only opened their homes and shared their stories, but put their trust in the central idea behind this book, sharing an authentic side of Byron—what it's really like to create a home and life here—beyond the cliches that often lack insight.

A special mention must also go to Delta Kay and Melissa Ladkin, for putting your trust in us and sharing your stories and wisdom.

Creating this book has been a wonderful gift in many ways, allowing us to connect with the people of our community on a deeper level. There's nothing quite like stepping inside someone's home to get to know them in a genuine way.

Similarly, working alongside a photographer for months on end is an immersive and educational experience. Thank you, Amelia, for joining me on this journey, for sharing your stories and creating the beautiful images in this book.

Special thanks also to designer Holly McCauley, as well as Jane, Roxy, Michael, Loran, Antonietta and the team at Hardie Grant.

Also, thank you once again to my team at Imprint House, including Holly, Phoebe and Sarah, for helping the business thrive while I spent time working on this book.

Finally, to Daniel, for always being my greatest champion and biggest support crew. And to Charles, Sabina, Isis and Miles; I'm so grateful that we all get to call Byron Bay home. My love for you all is limitless. Thank you for your patience, once again.

# Local production

This book has been a local production. In the spirit of celebrating and supporting community, the creators—the photographer, designer and author—can be found in the following ways:

## AMELIA FULLARTON
**Photographer**
@ameliafullarton
ameliafullarton.com

---

## HOLLY McCAULEY
**Designer**
@hollymccauley
hollymccauley.com
@yeahnice_gallery
yeah-nice.com

---

## NATALIE WALTON
**Author**
@nataliewalton
nataliewalton.com
@imprint_house
imprinthouse.net

# Learn more

## arakwal.com.au

Learn more about the culture of the Arakwal People.

———————————

## byronbaybook.com

*Byron Bay: The History, Beauty and Spirit*
by Peter Duke

A collection of photographs and stories about the history of Byron Bay, curated by Peter Duke.

———————————

## byronbayhistoricalsociety.org.au

Gain an insight into the history of the region through archival images and stories. A volunteer organisation, affiliated with the Royal Australian Historical Society.

## byrontrails.com

*Byron Trails: 50 Walking Adventures in Byron Bay* and *Beyond* by Mairéad Cleary

Discover walking trails throughout the region.

———————————

## nationalparks.nsw.gov.au/visit-a-park/ parks/arakwal-national-park

Jointly managed by the Arakwal People of Byron Bay and the NSW National Parks and Wildlife Service.

———————————

## Welcome to Country: A Travel Guide to Indigenous Australia

2nd edition by Marcia Langton (Hardie Grant)
A landmark guide to Indigenous Australia, offering insight into Australia's First Peoples, by a respected scholar and author.

# Resources

*An alternative way to explore Byron Bay*

Here is the locals' guide to exploring Byron Bay, based on the recommendations of those featured in this book.

———————

## FAVOURITE BEACHES

Alex Bennett: The Pass and Whites

Amelia Fullarton: No favourite—love them all!

Candice Rose-O'Rourke: All of them

Chelsea Waddell: Little Wategos

Claudia Martin: The Pass

Delta Kay: Broken Head

Erin Lovell Verinder: Torakina for a calm dip, or the Brunswick River at high tide: some days it turns aqua blue and could be mistaken for the Mediterranean

Gary Gorrow: All of them. It depends on the swell, the banks, crowds, winds and time of day

Hannah Fewson: Whites or Kings in Byron. The beach we can take cars and kids and dogs to at Lennox Head. Wategos. Belongil, because it's easier to park and you can get a margarita at the Treehouse afterwards

Heidi Daburger: Belongil Beach

Holly McCauley: Wategos has my heart

Jessica Blume: I love Wategos and Broken Head; they are my favourites. I like to surf at Tallows because I'm goofy

Lara Fells: Wategos

Louella Boîtel-Gill: Snorkelling at Clarkes Beach if it's hot. The wobbegongs and turtles are just amazing

Mel Ladkin: Tallows, Wategos, Captain Cook

Natalie Walton: The Pass is a family favourite. Everyone's happy!

Sally McGarry: The Pass, Wategos or Broken Head

Sonya Marish: Belongil

Victoria Aguirre: The Pass and Boulders

Zana Wright: Christmas Beach in a northerly wind; Little Wategos at five in the morning in a southerly with good sand banks

———————

## FAVOURITE WALKS

Alex Bennett: The lighthouse loop

Amelia Fullarton: Minyon Falls

Anna-Karina Elias: Pick any place to visit! It is all beautiful. Go to the Channon and walk the trails through the forest and feel the energy. Swim in the creeks and rivers and listen to the water. Feel the earth beneath your feet. Learn about Bundjalung Country, learn about the traditional owners of this abundant land and learn about the land itself. Listen to the stories of our First Nations People

Candice Rose-O'Rourke: The lighthouse walk

Chelsea Waddell: Minyon Falls bush walk

Claudia Martin: The lighthouse walk

Erin Lovell Verinder: A long stroll on Belongil Beach to pat all the smiling beach dogs

Gary Gorrow: I have a few but I keep them secret. Byron still has gems

Hannah Fewson: Minyon Falls loop through the ancient rainforest

Holly McCauley: Hell's Hole

Jessica Blume: I love walking around Upper Wilsons Creek, and the Mill Road. Protesters Falls is a beautiful walk, too

Lara Fells: The lighthouse walk

Louella Boîtel-Gill: Solo or without the dog is Broken Head. I love the fact you can nestle yourself in a sand dune and feel there's no one else in the world. Wategos is always a winner, especially swimming with my girls. I walk my dog, Lewis, on Belongil or Tallows at Suffolk

Mel Ladkin: Broken Head Nature Reserve; Nightcap National Park; Border Ranges National Park

Natalie Walton: Most weeks I do the lighthouse walk with a friend. It's good for the heart, mind and body

Sally McGarry: The lighthouse walk

Sonya Marish: From Belongil Beach and back into town

Victoria Aguirre: Arakwal National Park; Lennox Head to Boulders Beach

Yvonn Deitch: The lighthouse walk when visiting, but I would recommend Explore Byron Bay with local Indigenous woman Delta Kay

Zana Wright: Koonyum Range

———————————

**ALSO**

Amelia Fullarton: When it's raining, try to book snorkelling or kayaking out to Julian Rocks. It's in the water that Byron really shines

Erin Lovell Verinder: The farmers' markets offer the most incredible bounty of locally grown produce. My favourites are Friday morning at Mullumbimby or the charming little Saturday morning Bangalow farmers' market

Claudia Martin: The river in Brunswick for a picnic, or a kayak

Gary Gorrow: Sunrise on the beach. Farmers' markets. National parks

Hannah Fewson: Nightcap National Park

Jessica Blume: Christmas Beach at high tide: the Brunswick River turns turquoise and you can sit in the shade

Mel Ladkin: It is so very important to know whose land you are on, wherever you are. This land is ancient: it holds memory and wisdom; there is so much to learn. Be still, respect, ask questions and listen deeply

Natalie Walton: Spend time in the villages of the hinterland. Each one has its own character and many of the community halls host a food night once a week

Sonya Marish: Go for a drive out to the Channon and Nimbin markets to taste how things used to be in the Shire. It still has some of the authenticity of this area. The drive out there is so beautiful, too

Victoria Aguirre: Get to know which beaches are protected on windy days. You'll be surprised how beautiful a sheltered beach can be on what might otherwise seem a disaster of a day

Yvonn Deitch: Walk in the forest and swim in a waterhole. Explore the hinterland, go for a drive, take in the scenery and stop at road stalls for Davidson plum jam and finger limes, or whatever is in season

Zana Wright: Mullumbimby Community Gardens; Tweed Regional Gallery; Minyon Falls

# Acknowledgements

This book wouldn't have been possible without the following people. Many have local businesses and are actively involved in the Byron community. Take a look, and show your support.

**ALEX BENNETT**

Interior design consultant

@alex_bennett_design

———————————

**ANNA-KARINA ELIAS**

Ceramicist

@annakarinae

———————————

**CHELSEA WADDELL**

Joints in Byron

@jointsinbyron

airbnb.com.au/rooms/49618144

———————————

**CLAUDIA MARTIN**

Food stylist

@dreamingclaudia

———————————

**DELTA KAY**

Explore Byron Bay

@explore_byronbay

explorebyronbay.com

byronpledge.com.au

———————————

**ERIN LOVELL VERINDER**

Herbalist and nutritionist

@erinlovellverinder

erinlovellverinder.com

**GARY GORROW**

Soma

@soma.byron

somabyron.com.au

———————————

**HANNAH FEWSON**

Paddock Hall

@paddock_hall

@oneohseven_r

abnb.me/hRoVXlkuUeb

———————————

**HEIDI DABURGER**

Ha'veli of Byron Bay

@haveliofbyronbay

Haveli House

airbnb.com.au/rooms/9317450

Villa Jalan

abnb.me/fe0tao4jEcb

haveliofbyronbay.com.au

———————————

**JAMES LYELL**

Flight Facilities

flightfacilities.com

@flightfac

**JESSICA BLUME**

Jume

@shopjume

shopjume.com

Toko Toko

@shop.toko.toko

tokotokoworld.com

—————————————

**LARA AND MATT FELLS**

St. Agni

@stagnistudio

st-agni.com

@apartamento_byronbay

abnb.me/wY0UKyKaq3

—————————————

**LOUELLA BOÎTEL-GILL**

Interior designer

@louellaboitelgill

louellawhatever.com

@gypsycreekbangalow

—————————————

**MARTIN JOHNSTON**

Furniture maker

@martin_johnston_

martinjohnston.com.au

**MEL LADKIN**

Artist

@ochre.earth

ninbella.com/collections/melissa-ladkin

—————————————

**SALLY McGARRY**

@las_palmas_byron

laspalmasbyronbay.com.au

—————————————

**SONYA MARISH**

Jatana Interiors

@jatanainteriors

jatanainteriors.com.au

—————————————

**VICTORIA AGUIRRE AND CARL WILSON**

Pampa

@wearepampa

pampa.com.au

—————————————

**YVONN DEITCH**

@bytheseasidedaisies

—————————————

**ZANA WRIGHT**

Architect

@zanawright

zanawright.com

@make.hearth

Published in 2022 by Hardie Grant Books, an imprint of Hardie Grant Publishing

Hardie Grant Books (Melbourne)
Wurundjeri Country
Building 1, 658 Church Street
Richmond, Victoria 3121

Hardie Grant Books (London)
5th & 6th Floors
52–54 Southwark Street
London SE1 1UN

hardiegrantbooks.com

Hardie Grant acknowledges the Traditional Owners of the country on which we work, the Wurundjeri people of the Kulin nation and the Gadigal people of the Eora nation, and recognises their continuing connection to the land, waters and culture. We pay our respects to their Elders past and present.

A catalogue record for this book is available from the National Library of Australia

Home by the Sea
ISBN 978 1 74379 825 6
10 9 8 7 6 5 4 3 2 1

Publisher: Jane Willson
Project Editor: Antonietta Melideo/Loran McDougall
Editor: Jane Price
Design Manager: Kristin Thomas
Designer: Holly McCauley
Photographer: Amelia Fullarton
Production Manager: Todd Rechner

Colour reproduction by Splitting Image Colour Studio
Printed in China by Leo Paper Products LTD.

The paper this book is printed on is from FSC®-certified forests and other sources. FSC® promotes environmentally responsible, socially beneficial and economically viable management of the world's forests.